Autumn Manoeuvres

A Comedy in Two Acts

Peter Coke

A Samuel French Acting Edition

SAMUELFRENCH.COM
SAMUELFRENCH-LONDON.CO.UK

Copyright © 1983 by B.O.S. Ltd.
All Rights Reserved

Autumn Manoeuvres is fully protected under the copyright laws of the United States of America, the British Commonwealth, including Canada, and all other countries of the Copyright Union. All rights, including professional and amateur stage productions, recitation, lecturing, public reading, motion picture, radio broadcasting, television and the rights of translation into foreign languages are strictly reserved.

ISBN 978-0-573-11010-8

www.SamuelFrench.com
www.SamuelFrench-London.co.uk

FOR PRODUCTION ENQUIRIES

UNITED STATES AND CANADA
Info@SamuelFrench.com
1-866-598-8449

UNITED KINGDOM AND EUROPE
Theatre@SamuelFrench-London.co.uk
020-7255-4302

Each title is subject to availability from Samuel French, depending upon country of performance. Please be aware that *Autumn Manoeuvres* may not be licensed by Samuel French in your territory. Professional and amateur producers should contact the nearest Samuel French office or licensing partner to verify availability.

CAUTION: Professional and amateur producers are hereby warned that *AUTUMN MANOEUVRES* is subject to a licensing fee. Publication of this play(s) does not imply availability for performance. Both amateurs and professionals considering a production are strongly advised to apply to Samuel French before starting rehearsals, advertising, or booking a theatre. A licensing fee must be paid whether the title(s) is presented for charity or gain and whether or not admission is charged. Professional/Stock licensing fees are quoted upon application to Samuel French.

No one shall make any changes in this title(s) for the purpose of production. No part of this book may be reproduced, stored in a retrieval system, or transmitted in any form, by any means, now known or yet to be invented, including mechanical, electronic, photocopying, recording, videotaping, or otherwise, without the prior written permission of the publisher. No one shall upload this title(s), or part of this title(s), to any social media websites.

For all enquiries regarding motion picture, television, and other media rights, please contact Samuel French.

Please refer to page 64 for further copyright information.

CHARACTERS

Dame Beatrice Appleby, DBE (Bee)
Miss Elizabeth Hatfield (Hattie)
Miss Nanette Parry (Nan)
Brigadier Albert Rayne, CB, CMG, MVO
Mrs Ada Marlborough
Miss Blanche Meadows
Mrs Seymour Williams
Mrs Maxine Mayer
Yellow Jim
A Woman

The action takes place in the drawing-room of Dame Beatrice's flat overlooking the Albert Memorial, London

Time — the present

ACT I SCENE 1 Morning
        SCENE 2 A month later. Noon

ACT II   Two months later. Afternoon

ACT I

Scene 1

The overcrowded but delightful drawing-room of Dame Beatrice's old-fashioned flat overlooking the Albert Memorial in London. Morning

There are large bay windows, a single door leading to Bee's bedroom, and double doors leading to the hall, across which can be seen the front door. There are chairs, a sofa, a desk, a table and chairs, a small table and a great many interesting articles and objets d'art

As the Curtain *rises, cries of "Help!" are heard. Dame Beatrice Appleby, DBE (Bee) — well on in years, but with tremendous vitality and charm — is standing on a high stool at the window. She calls again*

Bee Help! Help! (*She pauses to listen*) Deaf idiots. (*Calling*) Emergency! SOS. Au secours!

There is a light tapping on the double doors, and Miss Hatfield — Hattie — a timid, bird-like little woman, puts her head round the door

Hattie Are you all right, Dame Beatrice?
Bee No, I'm not all right! Come and help me down.
Hattie (*coming in*) I thought I'd heard a sort of shouting for some time, but imagined it was the wireless.
Bee No, me. Suffering from cramp.
Hattie Oh, you poor thing.
Bee I don't want sympathy, I want your arm, come on.
Hattie Oh, yes, of course; I'm so sorry.

She helps her down

Bee That's better; thank you, Hattie. I felt like Nelson on his monument.
Hattie Were you trying to see something?
Bee No; I've at last got a new cleaning woman coming to be interviewed. I was trying to persuade the spiders to suspend work.
Hattie What a shame: I love spiders' webs.
Bee So do I. (*Wistfully*) And I really rather like the bloom of dust. (*Starting to dust*) But any decent daily would think we were stark staring mad. I hear this one's rather glum, but so long as she has strong arms who cares whether she smiles.
Hattie Let me help. (*Picking up a cloth*) I'm a very careful duster.
Bee That'd be most kind, dear. Don't bother to move anything: just a flick and dab job.

They go round dusting

Hattie Actually I'm glad to have a moment alone with you, Dame Beatrice. (*Hesitatingly*) I have something a little—awkward to tell you.
Bee Has the Brigadier been taking all the hot bath water again?
Hattie (*nodding*) And leaving puddles all over the floor. But that wasn't what I was going to say. It's not a complaint; more of a—plea.
Bee You're going to be late with the rent again?
Hattie However did you know? (*In a rush*) I am so sorry; I feel awful when you let me have the room so reasonably, but although I've new specs my china-mending's fallen terribly behind-hand. Still a client's brought me a splendidly broken Dresden dish—scores of pieces—and as soon as she pays, so shall I.
Bee (*patting her*) Don't think any more about it, dear. I know——

A firm knock on the door

Yes?

Nan—Miss Nanette Parry—a gaunt, late middle-aged woman with a deep voice, comes in

Nan I'm sorry to bother you, Dame Beatrice——(*She breaks off in annoyance as she sees Hattie*) Oh!
Bee Yes, Nan?
Nan Well, actually, it was a little business I wanted to discuss (*with a glance at Hattie*) in private.
Hattie Oh, then I'd better——
Bee You'd certainly better not. You're doing a wonderful job. (*To Nan*) If it's the—business I imagine it is, I assure you Hattie will completely sympathize.
Nan Oh, very well. (*Directly*) It's no good beating about the bush: I shall have to be a few days late paying for my room.
Bee Which means I shall have to be late paying the telephone, gas and electric bills.
Nan I realize it's very regrettable——
Bee The point is will the services be put off with just regrets?
Nan It's a great deal their fault. (*Pointing to the TV*) That damn box has ruined the art of speech. (*Accusing the set*) They mumble and slur and mispronounce till I could kick them. (*She kicks the set*) Oh, no harm, I hope. But it's infuriating. The few pupils who still come look on me as an old fogy whose love of beauty of voice is as old-fashioned as my hair-style. (*Very upset*) That's what one of them actually said to me!
Hattie (*putting her arm round her*) How wicked.
Bee (*doing likewise*) You teach and speak beautifully. (*Comfortingly*) None of them will ever have the success you had as an actress.
Nan (*mollified*) I did have one or two very good notices.
Bee Wonderfully versatile, everyone says.
Nan If you could have seen me as Cleopatra!
Bee (*slightly taken aback*) I'm sure we'd have been staggered.

Act I, Scene 1

The door opens, and Brigadier Albert Rayne CB, CMG, MVO — well over seventy, but with military bearing and charming manners, when he isn't being irascible — comes in

Brigadier A matter of urgency to discuss with you, if I may, Beatrice.
Bee Dear Mother! Not another?
Brigadier I beg your pardon?
Bee You're going to be late with the rent.
Brigadier Certainly not! Have I ever been late with the rent?
Bee (*nodding*) On more than one occasion.
Brigadier (*after a moment's confusion*) Due to oversight only. And immediately remedied.
Bee So what is it, Bertie?
Hattie (*moving to the door*) Perhaps it'd be better if we——
Brigadier (*interrupting*) No, no. It concerns you two; in a manner of speaking.
Nan (*darkly*) I somehow feel it's a manner we're not going to like.
Brigadier (*showing a letter*) I've just had this letter from an old army pal. Splendid chap, but is being turned out of his little flat, and has absolutely nowhere to go.
Nan Why doesn't he move to another little flat, Brigadier?
Brigadier (*bitterly*) Because, like me, he commuted his pension foolishly, and is now as broke as I am.
Bee So?
Brigadier What I just wondered——
Bee (*interrupting*) Was whether I'd give up my drawing-room to him? The answer is "No".
Brigadier I never for a moment considered that.
Nan (*ominously*) We wait anxiously for what you did consider, Brigadier.
Brigadier Well — (*with much clearing of throat*) — it's only a licked finger held up to the wind — but as you two ladies have very reasonably sized rooms——
Hattie (*strongly*) No!
Nan I think it impudence to suggest it.
Brigadier (*barking*) I haven't suggested it yet!
Nan If there's any room sharing you can do it with your army pal.
Brigadier How can I? As it is I have to close my desk before I can get into bed.
Hattie Privacy is the one luxury left in my life, Brigadier. I'm not brave, but would certainly fight for it.
Nan As would I. With tooth and nail.
Bee In any case, I'm afraid I have my own long list of desperate friends waiting to move in. (*Worriedly*) It's quite awful when one gets old with hardly a penny. Nobody wants one, and what places there are charge quite exorbitantly.
Hattie Oh, I know! I have an old friend who used to be a governess. She now can't afford the rent-rise, and has tried everywhere. I feel quite ill when I think about her.
Nan What about my old pal, Ella? A saint if ever there was one. Devoted her life to others, and now faces being stuck in a geriatric ward.

Bee Poor dear. (*Shaking her head worriedly*) Yes, we really ought to do something. If we who understand the awful difficulties don't help, who is going to? (*Looking round the room*) The trouble is that with the only exit from my bedroom through here——

Brigadier It'd be like Piccadilly Circus. Impossible.

Hattie Oh dear, you make me feel selfishly guilty. (*A little piteously*) There's really no real reason I shouldn't share my room——

Bee That's sweet of you, Hattie, but you'd also have to share a bath. And with only the four of us the water's never more than lukewarm.

Brigadier Yes, you're right, Beatrice: the flat's too small for more. (*Thoughtfully*) But all this has given me an idea. Only an idea, mark you——

Nan Oh dear, not another licked finger?

Brigadier (*ignoring her*) Is there something in the thought of an — annexe, so to speak?

Bee Explain, Bertie?

Brigadier Well, what — very vaguely — entered my head, is the flats that are about to become vacant in this block.

Hattie (*excitedly*) The one underneath this is marvellous!

Brigadier But enormous. What I had more in mind is – (*pointing*) – that foreign woman's next door.

Nan Mrs Spanager?

Brigadier Spanager, that's it. She's going to sell the remainder of her lease.

Bee Don't I know. She's always trying to get me to buy rubbish she doesn't want to pack. She left a Chinese coat thing here only yesterday.

Hattie Hers is a very nice flat.

Nan (*enthusiastically*) And as our friends wouldn't need a drawing or dining-room there'd be five bedrooms.

Hattie (*thrilled*) Think! We could take in five of the most deserving cases.

Bee Can you also think where the money's coming from to buy the flat?

As they all look dismayed, the front doorbell rings

Oh, dear Mother, that'll be Mrs Marlborough.

Brigadier Who?

Bee Mrs Marlborough, the new possible daily. Quickly, she mustn't see all the cleaning things . . .

They bustle about hiding them

Hattie Where shall I——

Bee Anywhere. The bucket, Bertie: behind the curtain. There I think that's all right.

The bell goes again

Nan We'd better skidaddle.

Bee No, no, she's reported to be difficult, stay and help. Bertie, be a dear: let her in so she gets a good first impression.

Brigadier (*delightedly going into the hall to the front door*) Certainly, certainly.

Bee Settle, and look as if we didn't know what a duster was.

Act I, Scene 1 5

They all sit nonchalantly. The Brigadier opens the front door

Brigadier Good-morning. Go straight in, will you?

Mrs Marlborough marches in. She is a forbidding, untidy woman

Mrs Marlborough (*having looked round. Flatly*) Oh. (*Then shaking her head firmly*) No. (*She turns to go*)
Bee One moment, Mrs Marlborough. Why exactly "No"?
Mrs Marlborough I've never cleaned in a museum. And I'm not starting now.
Bee There's really not as much as it looks. Do sit down and let's discuss it.
Mrs Marlborough I'd rather stand, thanks. So I can see surfaces. (*Drawing in her breath through her teeth as she peers*) No, no, no. Just this room would take 'ours.
Bee The last lady found it quite easy once she got into a routine.
Mrs Marlborough (*nastily*) She didn't clean the copper or brass, I see.
Bee It'll be lovely if you can.
Mrs Marlborough (*quietly challenging*) And what else would you expect?
Bee Well, there's this room, my small bedroom, the hall and the kitchen.
Mrs Marlborough Oh, this lot don't live 'ere, then?
Brigadier This lot do live here, but look after their own rooms.
Mrs Marlborough But have six large feet tramping in and out with dirt on them. What about a bathroom? I suppose you 'ave one. Am I to clean the grime-rim and toothpaste splatters?
Bee You are.
Mrs Marlborough (*grimly*) I see. And there's lots of rubbish to be 'umped down to some old yard, I expect?
Bee Yes.
Mrs Marlborough (*echoing*) Yes. And you'd like the silver given a rub now and then?
Bee Yes.
Mrs Marlborough (*echoing again*) Yes. And some veg peeled and left ready?
Bee Yes.
Mrs Marlborough Yes. And perhaps a few smalls to be rinsed through?
Bee Yes.
Mrs Marlborough Yes. (*Heavily sarcastic*) And what were you thinking of paying for these little duties?
Bee What do you suggest?
Mrs Marlborough (*nastily*) Plenty! Because I don't like being conned.
Bee Conned?
Mrs Marlborough Called in to look after a place what obviously 'asn't 'ad a good clean for months. Your "last lady"! You 'aven't 'ad one for years; any fool can see. And now 'ope I'll get it spotless so you can give me the sack and let it rot again till you call in the next dope. Well, you find 'er dear, because she's not Mrs Ada Marlborough.
Bee (*calmly*) I see. Well, Mrs Ada Marlborough, although we are rather well into the autumn of life, it does not mean that we're helpless; or fools, or prepared to be insulted by someone equally autumnal——

Mrs Marlborough 'Ere! You be careful what you say.
Bee I am. Otherwise I'd put it very differently.
Mrs Marlborough (*strongly*) Queen Victoria's dead, you know. People have *clear* rooms now, easy to clean. And even they can't get no-one. I've 'alf a dozen I can start with tomorrow. Including a TV star! Begging for a few 'ours she is.
Nan If I were you, I'd give in.
Mrs Marlborough (*furiously*) I'm not staying 'ere to be given advice by the lodgers.
Brigadier (*standing in her way*) You are, you know. You're staying here as long as we choose.
Mrs Marlborough (*suddenly slightly uncertain*) What the 'ell do you mean?
Brigadier (*forcefully*) What the hell I say! Sit down, woman. Immediately!

Nonplussed by his military tone, she sits. They gather round her

Now you listen to us for a change.
Mrs Marlborough 'Ere, half a mo——
Hattie No, no mos at all. Tell us first; what do you do with your dog when you're out working?
Mrs Marlborough 'Ow d'you know I've a dog?
Hattie Leave him alone and tied up all day, I expect.
Mrs Marlborough Well, I can 'ardly take him with me, can I?
Hattie (*jotting on a pad*) I'll get my friend in the RSPCA to look into it.
Mrs Marlborough Don't you dare send no-one like that to my place.
Nan What about his licence?
Mrs Marlborough What about it?
Nan (*jotting down*) My department is stepping up action against licence-dodgers.
Brigadier I fancy my department will be interested in seeing your television licence, too.
Mrs Marlborough (*too quickly*) I've got one, I've got one.
Brigadier Well, they'll soon check up.
Nan You declare your wages to the Inland Revenue, I'm sure?
Mrs Marlborough (*after hectic thought*) Mr Marlborough does all that.
Nan Your friend Milly in the Tax Office could soon verify, Dame Beatrice?
Bee Sure. (*Moving to the phone*) I'll give her a ring.
Mrs Marlborough No! Don't do that   (*swallowing*)   Madam. We may not be absolutely up to date.
Bee (*approaching her*) What a sweet little brooch you're wearing, Mrs Marlborough. Real diamonds?
Mrs Marlborough (*quickly covering it with her hand*) I've no idea.
Bee I have. I'm sure they're very good diamonds.
Mrs Marlborough (*after frantic thought*) A present from a lady I was with for years.
Bee (*ominously*) I'd like a brooch like that. I must ring round your employers, and find out where that lady bought it.

Mrs Marlborough looks at them as they stand grimly round her

Mrs Marlborough (*sulkily*) All right: you win. I'll come for two hours a day at what you paid the other, plus my fares.
Bee (*shaking her head*) You won't, Mrs Marlborough. You'll go. Immediately. And when you're next interviewed it might be as well to remember that white hair doesn't necessarily mean an addled head underneath. Goodbye!

The others stand back as Mrs Marlborough gets up truculently, and marches furiously towards the door

Slam that door as you go out, and the Post Office, Inland Revenue and RSPCA will all be on your door-step in the morning.

Mrs Marlborough very carefully opens the front door, and goes out closing it with extreme caution

Marvellous! Thank you so much, my dears. You supported me wonderfully.
Nan (*enthusiastically*) I enjoyed every moment.
Hattie We really showed her, didn't we?
Bee How did you guess about her dog, Hattie?
Hattie Hairs all down one side of her coat.
Bee Clever old Hattie.
Nan Spiffing how one idea seemed to lead to another.
Bee Yes, you were all very ingenious. (*Thoughtfully*) It's surprising what a banding-together like that can accomplish. Even if we are slightly more than twenty-one.
Brigadier I think that's rather the point, Beatrice. The young couldn't have dealt with her like that. She wouldn't have accepted it from them.
Nan Yes, you have something there, Brigadier. Although we senior citizens are not respected as we used to be, we're still regarded with a certain awe.
Bee I think because we've lived through so much.
Brigadier (*nodding*) Heard and seen so much—have such a fund of experience to draw on.
Bee (*thoughtfully*) Could remember back, and deal with any situation.
Brigadier Yes. (*Thoughtfully*) With any physical short-comings compensated by the authority and insight of rather a lot of years.
Hattie But doing what?

They all ponder on this

Brigadier (*quietly*) Doing something which means a great deal to all of us.
Hattie (*breathlessly*) What, Brigadier?
Brigadier (*slowly*) Getting hold of the flat next door for our friends.
Bee Oh, yes!
Hattie If only we could.
Nan It would be super.
Bee It certainly would.

They ponder again

Let's all sit down again, and put on our thinking caps.
Brigadier Wait a moment! (*Taking an envelope out of his pocket*) I'll jot down notes, and later assemble them under correct headings.
Nan We're not about to launch a bombardment, Brigadier.
Brigadier My first heading is "Object". Which is quite clear, isn't it? To annex the flat next door——
Nan (*nodding*) As an annexe.
Brigadier Now: "Method?"

They all sit blankly

Ideas please.
Bee I wasn't trained at the military academy but it seems perfectly clear that the only way to get the flat is to pay for it.
Brigadier Has anyone an alternative scheme?
Nan No.
Hattie No.
Brigadier Then I'll list suggestions of how we're to raise the money. (*Looking round*) First one?

There is no reply

Come along, come along, for goodness sake.
Nan It's a puzzle, isn't it?
Bee Well, we've called on our friends so often for other charities that it's no good going to them again.
Brigadier (*jotting down*) Then we must attack unknown persons.
Nan Unknown *rich* persons.
Brigadier Correct. Now who are the very wealthy nowadays?
Bee Judging from Harrods' sale there're still an astonishing amount of people with real money. Property tycoons for instance.

The Brigadier writes down each suggestion

Nan Pop stars, certainly.
Hattie House agents who sell expensive houses.
Brigadier Rolls-Royce owners. Yacht owners.
Bee Nobel prize-winners.
Nan Harley Street specialists.
Bee Dentists.
Hattie Undertakers?
Bee Not them, Hattie dear. Some of us are rather too near being customers.
Brigadier But the rest are a nice start. Now: how to get in touch with them?
Nan And make sure, of course, that they're really rich. A mink coat can go home to beans on toast.
Brigadier Yes, we have to penetrate their homes and businesses, and find out the real facts. How?
Hattie Impossible.
Brigadier I can't think Wellington's generals ever used that word to him, Miss Hatfield.

Act I, Scene 1　　　　　　　　　　　　　　　　　　　　　　　　　　　　9

Nan I don't suppose the poor beasts would have gone into battle at all against such odds.
Hattie (*pondering*) How to get in touch with the rich.

They all think

Brigadier Any suggestions?

He looks at them in turn. They each shake their heads. But Bee suddenly turns her shake into a frantic nod

Bee Yes, I have it, I have it! Mrs Ada Marlborough.
Brigadier Who the hell's she?
Bee The daily we put to flight.
Hattie She wouldn't have any money!
Bee But she's our solution. (*Slowly*) Bad and rude as she obviously is, she could get work in any home, or shop, or anywhere that's dusty.
Nan Everywhere in fact! Of course!
Hattie (*excitedly*) Oh, yes.
Brigadier I don't see the connection.
Hattie I do! To find out about rich persons we get into their houses by going as chars.
Nan Spiffing, Dame Beatrice!
Brigadier I am certainly not going out as a char!
Bee No, you'll have to be a butler or footman.
Brigadier (*indignantly*) I will do nothing of the sort!
Bee Do you want your army friend turned out on the street?
Brigadier No, poor chap. (*Thoughtfully*) I suppose I might possibly pass in an embassy or the like.
Bee Perfect. You'd be surrounded by exactly the – donors we're looking for.
Hattie I'm not absolutely clear, once we've found them, how we get them to – donate?
Bee We can't think of everything at once. We'll have to sort of – fit the action to the circumstances as we find them out.
Brigadier But we must be guided by proved military procedure. . . .

The telephone rings

Bee No, we mustn't. (*Going to the phone*) You've got to forget gunpowder, and think nuclear, Bertie. (*Into the phone*) Hullo? Oh, hullo, Mrs Spanager. . . . Yes. . . . Oh, really. Oh! Wait a moment, will you. (*Covering the receiver*) Get that Chinese coat which is on my bed will you?

Hattie flies out to the bedroom

(*Into the phone*) I beg your pardon, Mrs Spanager: I thought I smelt gas.

Hattie flies back with the coat

Oh, wait another moment. (*In a whisper to the others*) What do you think of it?
Hattie Lovely.

Nan Spectacular.
Brigadier Very good. A Chinese Mandarin's coat.
Bee How do you know?
Brigadier These dragons and flaming pearls. Saw masses of them when I served out East.
Bee Splendid. (*Into the phone*) So sorry to keep you waiting: not gas—just a bit of forgotten Stilton cheese. Now: I've got a better idea. You're far too— nice: he'll make rings round you. Let him look at your other things, then send him round here—not saying what about—and we'll deal with him for you. (*She listens*) Not at all: we'll enjoy it. Goodbye. (*She puts down the phone*) Mrs Spanager's got a dealer coming to buy things she's not taking. (*Excitedly*) A marvellous opportunity to test our powers by getting her a top price for this coat.
Nan Spiffing!
Brigadier No, no, you're jumping the gun, Beatrice.
Nan When's this man coming?
Bee He's due with her any moment.
Hattie (*panicking*) That doesn't give us time . . .
Brigadier We must have a plan.
Bee Get it down, then: "Operation Mandarin".
Nan Have you any idea what to ask?
Bee She took it to Sotheby's last year, and they said between fifty and eighty pounds.
Hattie As much as that?
Brigadier More, I guess. The dragon has five toes: it's probably royal.
Bee Bertie, you're marvellous. So marvellous you can be the one who's wearing it.
Brigadier Don't be absurd! Why on earth should I wear a thing like that in the middle of the morning?
Nan Why should any of us be wearing it at this time of the morning?
Hattie (*excitedly*) He doesn't know we're early risers: we could be one of those women who get up very late.
Bee Excellent, Hattie. You come in wearing it——
Hattie (*horrified*) Oh, I didn't mean I wanted to be the one! And what would I come in for?
Bee You can think of that. Then I mention buying it so that he knows it's for sale.
Nan Isn't that what he's coming for?
Bee No, I told her not to tell him. He'll be much keener if he thinks he's discovered something we hadn't thought of selling. (*Thinking it out*) We must start with another object . . .
Hattie (*looking round*) What about your clock?
Bee I couldn't possibly let him have that! My darling husband gave it to me. Besides, the little man who cleans it says it's worth a hundred pounds.
Nan Spiffing! Just what we want. He comes in, and you offer it to him——
Bee (*interrupting*) I do not!
Nan Half a jiff. You hint that you'll let it go cheaply——
Bee I won't.

Act I, Scene 1

Nan —Hattie arrives with the Chinese robe, and we divert attention to that. He buys it at a good price: (*emphasizing*) to please us so we'll sell him the clock. Then we get out of selling him the clock.
Brigadier How?
Nan (*crossly*) By thinking instead of asking subversive questions.

There is a long ring at the front door

Brigadier My God, it's him!
Hattie Oh, no! I've only the vaguest idea of my part.
Bee (*to the Brigadier*) You and Hattie'd better listen outside the door so you'll hear what's happening.
Hattie (*frantically*) How do I know when to come in?
Bee I'll ring this little hand-bell. First time for you, Hattie. Second for you, Bertie.
Brigadier What do I do?

The front doorbell rings again

Bee Not be found here for a start.
Brigadier Thank God for that.

He hurries out

Hattie (*also hurrying out*) Oh dear. Talk about wishing the earth would swallow you . . .
Bee Here! You'll swallow the whole enterprise without this.
Hattie (*grabbing the robe*) Oh, yes. Oh dear, oh dear . . .

She exits

Nan I'd better let him in.
Bee Yes. (*Rushing to get a duster*) I'll be dusting to put him off the tack.
Nan Why should it do that?
Bee No idea. But it'll stop him seeing my hands trembling.

She dusts furiously as Nan opens the front door

Blanche Meadows comes in. She has dyed hair, odd clothes, and an ingratiatingly confidential manner that doesn't completely hide her sharpness

Bee and Nan both stare at her

Blanche (*in her soft cooing voice*) Good-morning.
Bee Good-morning. Are you him?
Blanche I beg your pardon, dear?
Bee No, I beg yours. We were expecting - someone else. What can I do for you?
Blanche Mrs Spanager suggested I popped in.
Nan So you are him.
Blanche I beg?
Bee Take no notice: we're a little disturbed. My friend just fell off a ladder. (*To Nan*) Go and sit down, dear. You'll feel all right in a moment.
Nan (*limping to a chair and sitting*) Yes, if nothing's broken.

Blanche I've obviously come at a bad moment. (*Starting to leave*) I'll return some other time.
Bee (*almost grabbing her*) No, no, no. She's making a lot of fuss about nothing; it was only off the first rung. Come and sit down, Mrs —?
Blanche Miss Meadows. But everyone calls me Blanche.
Bee I'm happy to meet you, Miss Blanche.

They both sit

What exactly did Mrs Spanager say?
Blanche That you might have something you wished to dispose of.
Bee (*very surprised*) Really? I don't remember telling her anything like that.
Blanche (*rising*) She must have got hold of the wrong end of the stick. (*Going to the door*) So sorry to have disturbed you.

Bee watches speechless

Nan Your memory's worse than mine, Dame Beatrice. That clock that loses time. That's what you said you were going to get rid of.
Bee Yes, of course: how silly of me. But I don't suppose an old clock would interest you, Miss Blanche.
Blanche (*trying to hide her interest*) Well, it's not really my line. But you never know, dear. Mind if I take a peep?
Bee You peep as much as you like.

Blanche carefully examines the clock while the other two look at each other anxiously

Blanche Yes. Quite nice, dear. Bits of damage, of course. (*Sadly shaking her head*) But it's really only big clocks that sell.
Bee Oh. (*She stretches out her hand to the bell*)
Blanche Mark you, all clocks are worth something.

Bee withdraws her hand

Everyone's got to know the time, haven't they? What sort of money had you in mind?
Bee I really don't know.
Blanche Well, I'll risk being able to get rid of it, and offer you — fifty pounds?
Bee Absurd; it's insured for a hundred.
Blanche (*coyly stern*) So you do have an idea what it's worth. Naughty! But d'you also know the insurance value is based on twice the market value? Still, I don't want to seem stingy. We'll split the difference: seventy-five.
Bee Well — let's have a cup of tea while we think about it . . . (*She rings the hand-bell*)
Blanche Oh, I haven't time for a cuppa, dear. Pardon me . . . (*She turns her back on them*) With all this mugging I keep my money pinned high.

Hattie comes in wearing the too-long Chinese robe

Bee (*pretending not to see her*) Bring tea, will you, Doris?
Hattie (*completely nonplussed*) Doris? Tea?
Bee Oh, it's not Doris! It's you, Miss Hatfield.

Act I, Scene 1   13

Hattie Yes, it is. Have I overslept?
Bee No, no; it's only about twelve.
Hattie Twelve? Oh, what a sleepy-head I am.

They look at Blanche waiting for her to comment. When she doesn't:

Bee But a very smart sleepy-head.

She looks at Blanche who continues counting notes

Nan (*emphasizing*) A really dazzling sleepy-head.

Blanche concentrates on her counting. Hattie yawns, and eventually in despair, starts to leave

Hattie Well – I suppose I'd better go.
Bee (*alarmed*) Where to?
Hattie (*at a loss*) Back to bed, I suppose. (*She walks towards the door*)
Bee Don't forget you promised me that old dressing-gown for my bazaar.
Hattie Oh, did I?
Bee You know you did.
Hattie Yes, of course I know I did! I'm still half asleep.

Blanche suddenly becomes alert

Blanche (*going to Hattie*) You're going to sell this?
Hattie No! I mean, yes. I mean – oh, I don't know what I mean. I'm so sleepy; I must go back to bed. (*Realizing*) Oh, but I can't, can I! (*With relieved inspiration*) Yes, I can – because I'm so hot. Feverish. I can't bear this old thing. (*She throws off the coat*) I'm going back to bed: I'm sure I've got sleepy sickness.

She flees in her night-dress

Bee (*to Blanche*) You must excuse her: I'm afraid she's a little too fond of the bottle.
Nan (*limping and picking up the coat*) But it's a colourful coat; you should do well out of it, Beatrice.
Bee Yes, I've one or two people interested already.
Blanche (*over-casually*) I might be interested actually. (*Examining it*) The thread's pulled here and there, but it's quite nice.
Bee Very nice. We've had expert advice.
Blanche As to price as well?
Bee Yes. (*Challengingly*) A hundred and fifty pounds.
Blanche (*pretending dismay*) Oh, surely not, dear? This is the sort of thing I do know about. I'd say a hundred'd be overdoing it.
Nan Ah, but charity buyers always pay a little more than it's worth.
Blanche (*after a moment*) So how much more would you consider?
Bee I suppose if you offered a hundred and forty ...
Blanche Well, as I'm buying the clock as well, what about a hundred and twenty-five?
Bee (*accusingly*) It's for charity, Miss Blanche! A hundred and thirty or no sale.

Blanche Oh, very well. (*Counting out notes*) I'll hardly make a penny, but it's a nice bit of stock. (*Offering the notes*) There you are: one hundred and twenty.

Nan is scribbling on a piece of paper in her notepad

Bee One hundred and thirty.
Blanche Oh, is that what we agreed? Silly me!

She gives Bee the money who puts it in one of her pockets

Nan (*handing her the paper on which she's been scribbling*) And if you'd be so kind?
Blanche What is it, dear?
Nan A receipt. (*Giving her the pen*) Just sign there, if you will.
Blanche (*reluctantly*) I don't really like signing things. I pass articles on so quickly and with so little profit I can't afford VAT and all that on top.
Bee It's only for our fussy charity accountant.
Blanche Oh, all right, dear. (*She scribbles on it, and puts it in Bee's pocket*) There; you can feel safe.
Bee Thank you so much.
Blanche Now let's settle the clock equally easily, dear. Seventy we agreed, didn't we?
Bee Seventy-five. But thinking it over——
Blanche (*interrupting*) Oh, seventy-five: what a silly I am this morning. Seventy-five it shall be then ...

She starts counting out the money. They watch in alarm. Bee frantically rings the hand-bell

Bee Where on earth is that wretched Doris?
Blanche (*holding out notes*) Here you are, dear.

As Bee stands helpless the Brigadier bursts in

Brigadier Splendid news, Beatrice.
Bee It needs to be. What is it?
Brigadier (*handing her a cheque*) A cheque for a hundred and fifty pounds.
Bee A hundred and fifty pounds! For what?
Brigadier Your clock, of course. You told me to sell it. I have.
Nan Brilliant, Brigadier.
Bee Oh, Bertie, how clever!
Blanche One moment, dears. Is that the clock I'm buying?
Bee I'm so sorry; I'm afraid there's no question of that now.
Brigadier Yes, yes, he's written the cheque. It's the property of my (*emphasizing*) High Court Judge now.
Blanche But I only gave over the odds for the Chinese coat as I thought I was going to make a little bit on the clock——

Nan interrupts her with a loud groan

Bee Your leg hurting?
Nan No, something far worse.

Act I, Scene 1   15

Brigadier What?
Nan It's twelve o'clock! The monster will be here any moment.
Blanche The man who's bought the clock?
Nan No, no, no. Worse. From the Inland Revenue. To inspect my accounts.
Blanche (*horrified*) The VAT people?
Nan (*nodding*) A man like a hawk with eyes like screwdrivers.
Blanche (*very nervous*) He mustn't see me. He just might question me about my book-keeping. I have answers of course, but he mightn't completely understand. I think I'd better be off. (*Looking at the robe*) But I don't know I really want this now——
Bee (*pushing it at her*) Of course you do: it's royal. It'll be snapped up. (*Pretending to listen*) Is that the lift stopping at this floor?
Blanche I'll nip down the stairs. But it's all most unsatisfactory. (*Hurrying to the door*) I don't do business like this; I'll come in some other time. If he asks about me, you've never seen me before: I just came in selling poppies.

She scurries out of the front door

Nan A triumph! A veritable triumph.
Bee Well, there were one or two awkward moments, but you were wonderfully inventive, Nan. And you, Bertie.
Brigadier Lucky she didn't look at the cheque: it was one of mine.
Nan I thought we'd better get a receipt in case she tried to back out.
Bee (*taking the receipt from her pocket*) A brainwave, Nan. (*Looking at it*) Even if it mightn't hold up in a court of law.
Nan Why not?
Bee She's signed "Marie Antoinette"!

The door opens and Hattie puts her head round, still in her night-dress with a dressing-gown

Hattie Safe?
Bee Come in, Hattie dear, come in. You played your part wonderfully, too.
Hattie I didn't play anything. I was so frightened I really did feel ill. I'm still unusually hot.
Bee (*taking the notes from her pocket and waving them*) Let the sight of our gains cool you.
Nan Fifty more than Mrs Spanager's top hopes.
Hattie No! Miraculous.
Bee And far more important: wonderful proof that we're perfectly capable of carrying out a scheme if we really set our minds to it.
Hattie We are; we really are, aren't we?
Brigadier I have to admit it came off far better than I'd dared hope.
Hattie (*breathlessly*) So do we start going out as chars, and finding donors?
Bee (*nodding*) Providing they're very wealthy. Then all we'll be doing is manœuvring them into giving what they can very well afford, to those who very urgently need it.
Nan A spiffing way of looking at it! Ella will be over the moon when I tell her we can give her a room.
Brigadier My army pal must have the one nearest the bathroom: he has troubles.

Hattie (*anxiously*) My old governess friend will be seriously considered, won't she?
Bee (*nodding*) We'll draw up a list of possibles, and choose the most urgent.
Hattie I'll pop in every morning and evening to do little jobs for them.
Nan I'll always help out with shopping. And in the afternoons——
Brigadier Wait a minute, wait a minute! You're galloping away again before the flag.
Bee Yes. Let's get it quite clear first. We all agree we can, and must, have the annexe?
Hattie Oh, yes!
Brigadier If the greatest precautions are taken.
Nan We've got to: full stop.
Bee Then let's take the first irrevocable step!
Nan I agree.
Hattie The sooner the better.
Brigadier (*suspiciously*) What step, Beatrice?
Bee If we dither any longer we'll be put off by the cold. (*Moving to the phone and dialling*) Let's plunge.
Nan Into what?
Hattie Let's, whatever it is.
Nan Here, here.
Brigadier (*urgently*) No, no, you must liaise with us before taking action, Beatrice.
Nan Liaising with you takes so long, Brigadier.
Bee (*silencing them with a frantic wave. On the phone*) Mrs Spanager? Beatrice Appleby. I have good news. We've sold your Chinese coat for one hundred and thirty pounds. (*She listens*) I thought you would be. But wait a minute! I've even better news. (*Slowly and distinctly*) We've also sold your flat for you!

The CURTAIN *falls on their expressions of alarm and elation*

SCENE 2

The same. A month later. Noon

When the CURTAIN *rises, the Brigadier is placing four chairs round the table. He adds a carafe of water, four glasses, and a pile of papers and files. Then sitting centre, puts his pocket-watch on the table, takes a gavel from his pocket, and bangs*

Brigadier (*calling to the bedroom door*) Come along, Beatrice, come along. The meeting was scheduled for noon. It's now twelve-o-five.
Bee (*off*) Coming, Bertie.

She opens the bedroom door, and appears with an apron over her dress, with her hair done up in a gaudy handkerchief, a cigarette hanging from her mouth, and carrying dusters and polish

Act I, Scene 2   17

(*With an accent*) I want to 'oover so get your be'ind off of that chair.
Brigadier What on earth are you doing dressed up like that?
Bee (*dropping the accent and removing the handkerchief and apron*) Just trying it out. I mustn't become "known", so I thought I'd stop being Mrs Andrews, and become Mrs Lillywhite next job.
Brigadier But you can't leave your present family. Or have you found out enough already?
Bee No, no. But I'm considering taking an afternoon job as well.
Brigadier You'll do nothing of the sort; you'll wear yourself out.
Bee No, I shan't. Rich people's houses are extraordinary. I'm fascinated.
Brigadier You're not there to enjoy yourself, Beatrice; you're there to gather information. Anyhow, all this should only be discussed before the others. That's why we have these regular meetings. Where the hell are they? It's twelve-o-eight now.
Bee We dailies have to work elastic hours, Bertie. It's no good trying to control us with railway timetabling. (*She opens the bedroom door and throws in her "daily" bits and pieces*)
Brigadier (*huffily*) It's nothing to do with the railways. It's accepted military procedure.
Bee The military don't move their troops by underground, and the practically non-existent seventy-three bus.

Nan hurries in wearing a hat and coat

Nan Sorry to be a jiffy late. My poor beasts had a dinner-party for eight last night.
Bee Oh, poor Nan.
Nan They're so thoughtless. The washing-up's never stacked properly; just piled higgledy-piggledy so the first half-hour's spent disentangling.
Brigadier Why are you wearing that funny hat?
Nan (*crossly*) What's funny about it?
Brigadier I meant – it's funny seeing you wearing a hat.
Nan (*taking off her hat and revealing a turbaned head, and an apron beneath her coat*) How else do I get past the porter without him suspecting?
Bee What a good idea, Nan. I take a selection of good and bad scarves, and change in the bus. But I get some very odd looks.

Hattie taps and comes in, very distressed

Hattie I do apologize for being so late. But I've had a mishap.
Bee Oh, Hattie dear. Nothing serious?
Hattie Yes. (*She pauses*)
Brigadier Well, what, Miss Hatfield?
Hattie (*almost in tears*) I've got the sack!
Nan Oh, you poor beast.
Hattie Their horrid little child pinched me on my – where he shouldn't. I completely lost control, and slapped him.
Bee Probably did him a lot of good.
Hattie (*wailing*) But that I should do it! I who am such a strong voice against capital punishment.

Bee I'm sure I'd have done exactly the same. Only harder.

Brigadier (*nodding agreement*) Half the trouble with the world nowadays is that people like your rich film-magnate spoil their children so much. You've probably nipped a future mugger in the bud.

Nan It's also nipped our lovely free cinema tickets in the bud.

Bee So what? I haven't been able to enjoy my bath since that awful film where rats came up the plug-hole.

Brigadier (*impatiently*) Our scheduled meeting is eleven minutes late. Will you kindly take your places, ladies?

The ladies go to their chairs

Hattie (*as she sits*) I'm relieved not to go back in a way. They had mustard with everything: it's so difficult to wash off plates.

Nan Egg's my bugbear. Sticks like glue.

Bee Wait till you get bran! My lot have it with their breakfast cereal. Not only does it stick——

Brigadier (*banging his gavel*) Ladies, please! This is a Planning and Report Committee, not a Domestic Hints and Tips Bureau. (*Shuffling papers*) Now. Up to date our rather lin. ed operations have brought in only moderate financial gains. But they have been enormously valuable in the lessons we have learned. So let me stress that we must apply these lessons in the next two major schemes we are about to carry out.

Hattie I feel jellified to think of them.

Brigadier Quite unnecessary. Firstly—due to good scouting by Miss Parry——

Nan (*interrupting*) Oh, I can't accept all the praise. If it hadn't been for Dame Beatrice taking on that cleaning job at the showroom in Berkeley Square we'd never have had the list of Rolls-Royce owners to start us off.

Brigadier I agree; very commendable.

Hattie Oh, yes.

Bee (*shaking her head*) I should have stayed till I got more. But that marble floor and my knees——

Brigadier (*over-ridingly*) Firstly, then, we have "Operation Pop Star". By the way, Miss Parry, what do we call him to his face?

Nan Yellow Jim, of course.

Brigadier Hasn't he got a proper name?

Nan Alfie Tank. But he doesn't like it remembered. Now it's "Yellow Jim and His Junkies".

Brigadier Good God!

Hattie I caught a bit of him on television last night. I think he's marvellous. That sort of hysterical voice. I can't tell you what it does to me.

Brigadier I can tell you——

Bee (*interrupting*) I thought this was supposed to be a Planning Meeting?

Brigadier Yes, yes, you're quite right, Beatrice. (*To Nan*) You're completely satisfied this fellow can afford to—donate?

Nan Crippen, yes. The last bill for servicing his Rolls—just tightening the bolts or whatever they do—was fifteen hundred pounds. And he never queried it.

Act I, Scene 2   19

Brigadier (*making note*) He can afford to donate. Good. So "Operation Pop Star" at fifteen hundred hours next Wednesday the twenty-fourth.
Hattie Our first really big operation! I feel swimmy. (*Firmly correcting*) No, I don't! I feel ice-cool with brain aflame.
Bee (*with raised eyebrows*) Good. Because it must be a success. It's over a month since we said we'd buy the flat, and Mrs Spanager hasn't even had a penny of the deposit.
Nan We've given her very good excuses. (*Innocently*) Anyone can make a mistake dating a cheque.
Bee But how much longer are such "mistakes" going to put her off? When I ran across her in Marks and Spencer's yesterday her smile was decidedly deep-freeze.
Brigadier (*crossly*) All the more reason to stick to the business in hand. (*Looking at papers*) Our second scheme—exact date and time yet to be decided—is Hattie's "Operation Beetle".
Hattie (*holding up her hand*) Is it in order to decide it now?
Brigadier Why?
Hattie I probably haven't stressed it enough before, but Mr Andropolous is very ancient. We don't want him popping off before we operate.
Bee We certainly don't.
Brigadier Then I'll pencil it for the following Wednesday, the first. Tomorrow I'll go over the route again with my stop-watch, and check timings. (*He makes a note*) Then we have our two semi-planned schemes: "Operation Centre Court" and "Operation Sleeping Beauty".
Nan (*demandingly*) What about my "Operation Racing Car"?
Bee We agreed it was too dangerous, Nan.
Nan I didn't agree.
Brigadier (*over-ridingly*) Even without "Operation Racing Car" we have a very nice little reserve of ideas. But as it's absolutely essential that neither we, nor the flat, can ever be traced and so investigated——
Nan Using each scheme only once surely there's no possible danger?
Brigadier (*witheringly*) Exactly the point I was trying to make, Miss Parry. But covering our tracks in so many different ways, so that there's no pattern to be followed, means ideas are used up rapidly. Therefore it is of paramount importance——
Bee (*interrupting*) To come to the crux of the matter without too much speechifying.
Brigadier (*huffily*) I am only trying to give the meeting a formal basis so that it doesn't disintegrate into—(*pointedly*)—unproductive washing-up waffle.
Nan (*irritated*) You'll please remember you're talking to the people who do the actual work, Brigadier.
Brigadier And I'll ask you to remember that it's not my fault I can't get jobs as easily as you do, Miss Parry.
Nan It's hardly anyone else's fault that at your first one you poured bread-sauce all over the chief guest.
Bee (*hastily*) That's all water under the bridge. What is it that's of "paramount importance", Bertie?

Brigadier (*heavily ironic*) That I stop "speechifying" obviously. I therefore hand over to the "workers". Perhaps in turn you'll give your ideas concerning any possible new benefactors, and any new possible schemes for persuading them to donate. (*He sits*)

Bee (*tactfully*) Put beautifully succinctly, Bertie. I shall try to copy you in my report. (*Standing*) Well, there's no doubt that my Lebanese family are "possibles". Mr Habib has just given each of his lady friends a most expensive small new car.

Brigadier Good God!

Nan I thought you said there was a Mrs Habib.

Bee There is: a sweet woman.

Hattie Poor creature.

Bee Not at all. Her one passion is her stables. She knows that every new mistress means a new horse so she couldn't be happier. Therefore I propose "Operation Lebanon" for the future, and will submit details when fully gathered. (*She sits down*)

Brigadier (*who has taken notes*) Operation accepted. Next, Miss Parry. Your report, please.

Nan (*standing*) Well, I'm enjoying being with my interior decorator off Bond Street no end. For one thing they have the most stupendous hoover. It simply whizzes across the carpets———

Bee (*warningly*) Nan! (*With a glance at the Brigadier*) I don't want you to be ruled out of order.

Nan Thanks. But I think I'm wasting my time: all the really expensive jobs we're undertaking are in the country. And as our only transport is Mr Ashmore———

Bee Oh yes! Do forgive me for interrupting, Nan, but I must bring up Mr Ashmore before I forget. It's so convenient him living downstairs, and he's so ready to drive us at any time of day or night, that I think perhaps we're exploiting him a bit. Should we consider giving him a little something more than just his petrol money?

Brigadier I thought you said he was perfectly happy with the pound of your home-made fudge every week?

Nan His complete discretion is vital to us.

Bee Oh, there's no doubt about that; he's even more excited about the annexe than we are.

Brigadier Still, perhaps we'd better be on the safe side. Increase the fudge-ration to a pound and a half. I'll note it.

Bee I'd much rather you helped me stir the wretched stuff.

Brigadier (*hastily*) So you think you'd better move to another job, Miss Parry?

Nan (*nodding*) I've already prepared the ground by telling them my husband is carrying on with a blonde———

Hattie Your husband!

Nan (*defensively*) Perfectly possible.

Bee (*placatingly*) Oh, very possible.

Nan So I think tomorrow I'll give in my notice saying I've ousted the blonde, so need time off to go on a second honeymoon.

Act I, Scene 2 21

Hattie You're marvellous, Nan.
Nan Thank you. Then I suggest moving to a Canadian family that my bus-stop friend Lil told me about. In furs. with three cars. (*She sits*)
Brigadier (*noting it down*) I think we'd certainly approve the move.
Hattie Hear, hear.
Bee (*nodding*) Very promising.
Brigadier Next.

They all stare at Hattie who is smiling happily to herself

Next!
Hattie (*jumping to her feet*) Oh, I'm so sorry. I was just having a vision of myself swathed in mink.
Brigadier (*severely*) Any Canadian furs would be put towards the annexe, Miss Hatfield, not on your back.
Hattie Oh, I know, I know. I'm so sorry. But it was a vision. It came to me: I couldn't help it.
Brigadier Your report.
Hattie Well, as you know, I mostly have only failure to report——
Bee Nonsense. Mr Andropolous and his beetle collection is going to be wonderfully profitable.
Nan God, and the Russians, willing.
Hattie But that awful film family were so beastly I'm afraid I concentrated on self-preservation rather than information.
Brigadier We can't expect to spot a winner every time. (*Consulting a list*) I think we'll send you to perfume. A wealthy French lady who is one of the top importers.
Hattie Oh, good. I love a rich smell! But wait a moment. What I wanted to say was that next door to the beastlies lives a real "possible".
Brigadier (*pen poised*) Details?
Hattie She's a Mrs Seymour Williams: a widow with a house stuffed with treasures who's so rich she has a TV in every room including the loos.
Bee How on earth do you know?
Hattie She has a sweet daily called Mary who's always asking me in when the old girl's out. We drink Earl Grey tea and eat hand-made biscuits from Fortnum and Mason's.
Nan Lucky beast. We only have stale ginger-nuts from the Co-op.

Bee, with a glance at the Brigadier, clears her throat

Hattie Oh, yes. Well, I think the way to get Mrs Seymour Williams to help us with the annexe is through her dogs.
Brigadier What on earth have dogs——?
Bee You may hear if you listen, Bertie.
Hattie She has two she simply adores. They're quite revolting—not their fault, poor dears, they're fed all day on chocolates and sponge-fingers—but I think can lead us to a small share of the Seymour Williams fortune.
Nan Spiffing.
Brigadier How?
Hattie Anyone who loves dogs like that is very vulnerable——

The telephone rings
Brigadier Damn! Let it ring.
Bee (*getting up*) Certainly not: might be something exciting. (*Into the phone*) Hullo? (*Her face falling*) Oh, hullo, Mrs Spanager. . . . Figures and writing on my second cheque don't agree? Oh, how silly of me! . . . Don't be ridiculous! It's my carelessness, nothing to do with fate! . . . You haven't!! But you've no right to! Mrs Spanager? (*Putting down the phone*) Damn woman's hung up on me.
Nan What, what?
Bee Says two bounced cheques means we're not fated to have the flat, so she's rung the agents and put it on the market.
Hattie No!
Brigadier The witch.
Nan Make it a "b", Brigadier.
Hattie (*frantically*) She mustn't be allowed to! We've got to have it for our friends. We've got to. They'll be destitute otherwise.
Bee What can we do? She's put it up for sale.
Nan (*firmly*) We must stop it somehow.
Hattie (*miserably*) You can't stop what's already been done.
Nan Then it'll have to be undone. (*Thinking*) How much do the agents know about her?
Bee Little, I'd guess. I've lived here thirty-five years, and they still look at me as if I'd just come off the Ark.
Nan Splendid. (*Crossing to the phone. To Bee*) You have the agents' number?
Bee On that letter in red. Their final demand for service charges.
Nan (*dialling*) You trust me?
Brigadier (*grudgingly*) Can't think of any alternative.
Nan (*into the phone, with a German accent*) 'Ullo? Put me bitte to flats for the sale, ya? (*Covering the receiver*) What's the number of Mrs Spanager's flat?
Bee Twenty-four.
Nan (*into the phone*) 'Ullo? Flats for the sale, ya? Frau Spanager has give to you her flat twenty-four for the sale, ya? . . . Ya. This here vas her dear daughter——(*covering the receiver and speaking in a frantic whisper*) German Christian name?
Bee Brunhilda.
Brigadier No, no, too fancy.
Nan (*into the phone*) 'Ullo? Vat a bat line. This vas Frau Spanager's dear daughter Hilda. Ve hov just arrive from Berchesgarten to stay mit lieber Mutter. And vill not hear of her to leave flat. (*Vehemently*) Nein, nein, nein! Ve vill pay all expenses, so please to cancel sale of flat. Ya? . . . Danke schoen. Auf Wiedershein. (*She puts down the phone*) Accent a bit ropey, I fear.
Bee But content vunderbar!
Brigadier Yes, well done, Miss Parry.
Hattie Yes, but will it stop her ringing them when no-one arrives to view?
Nan What about cutting her telephone wires?
Brigadier It'd mean taking the planks up in the corridor. Too dangerous.

Act I, Scene 2

(*Worriedly*) We've got an explosive situation. We must take the offensive quickly. Get down to the office, make an offer for the flat——
Hattie Nan's told them it isn't for sale!
Bee We can get round that by saying Hilda's potty. Will they ring Mrs Spanager back and confirm?
Brigadier Then we sign a provisional agreement then and there——
Bee (*flatly*) And haven't enough deposit to back it up.
Nan Curses!

They sit in despair for a moment

Hattie With all this money coming in from charring I have quite a nice little bit saved. I could spare nearly fifty pounds.
Bee That's sweet of you, Hattie. But if it's not to be suspicious we'll have to pay the whole amount. It is only the deposit.

They consider again in silence

Nan We're going to lose our flat you know.
Hattie But our poor friends! We simply must get somewhere for them.
Bee (*thoughtfully*) Are we being blind-folded by the thought of not getting the money till next Wednesday?
Brigadier Clarify, Beatrice.
Bee Mightn't it be possible to get the deposit money before then?
Nan Yes! Why shouldn't we do one of the other schemes straight away?
Brigadier Because they're not fully planned.
Bee Hattie's beetle scheme is all but planned.
Hattie Oh, heavens!
Brigadier (*sternly*) All but planned doesn't guarantee success.
Bee It's no good having a lovely guaranteed success when the flat's sold to someone else.
Nan And you've researched it so thoroughly, Brigadier. Any slight hitches can be overcome with natural invention.
Brigadier I wouldn't be at all happy——
Bee (*interrupting*) I would. Because it's our only possible chance. We'll vote. Those in favour of immediate action?

She shoots up her hand, as does Nan. Hattie timidly follows after they both stare at her

Bee Passed! Dig out the plans, Bertie.

The Brigadier sorts out papers on the table

Get Mr Andropolous on the phone, Hattie.
Hattie Now?
Bee Of course.
Hattie (*horror-stricken*) But I'd never have voted "yes" if I'd known I had to perform without a go-through first.
Nan (*comfortingly*) We will go through it while we wait for him to arrive. You can't let down our homeless friends.

Hattie (*after a moment*) You're right, I can't. I'd never forgive myself. All right. Give me the details, Brigadier, before my eyes go squinty.

Nan (*taking a paper from the Brigadier*) I'll dial the number for you. (*She does so*)

Hattie No, no, I must have time to think!

Brigadier (*giving her a paper*) There's nothing to think about: you have all the data there.

Nan No answer.

Hattie Thank goodness!

Bee But I thought you said he never went out?

Hattie He doesn't. But with any luck he has.

Nan He's answering! Quick! (*She pushes the receiver into Hattie's hands*)

Hattie Mr Andropolous? This is Mrs Hardcastle . . . Amy Hardcastle. Who cleaned for you a little while ago, and had to leave because of her gallstones. . . . Oh, they've melted, thank you. I'm ringing because the lady I told you about is most interested in the idea of exhibiting your beetle collection. She has a passion for beetles, and this large house in the country, and would love to discuss turning part of it into the Andropolous Museum. . . . I thought you might be. She wonders if you could come round and discuss any little financial arrangement? Only it'd have to be immediately as she's had a sudden tempting offer to turn the house into a health farm. (*She listens. Then covers the receiver, and speaks in a frantic whisper*) He's having his lunch.

Bee Then after lunch.

Hattie (*into the phone*) Then when you've finished your pudding. (*She listens. Then to the others*) Has to have his rest.

Brigadier Then after his damn rest.

Hattie (*into the phone*) When you wake up perhaps? . . . But if you wrapped up warmly. . . . Oh. Five-eight-nine six-two-two-two. (*She puts down the receiver*) He's snuffily, but will ring you when he's better.

Nan Curses!

Bee Fussy old idiot. Just the sort that gets the aged a bad name.

Hattie I'm really quite disappointed; I was so keyed up I could have done anything.

Nan We were all keyed up: it's damnable.

Bee (*after a moment*) No, it's not! As we're all emotionally geared, let's try again.

Brigadier Now be careful, Beatrice; I feel you're going to venture into a mine-field.

Bee Probably. We must just weave between the mines.

Brigadier Oh, my God!

Bee We have another operation ready, haven't we?

Hattie "Pop Star"?

Bee Exactly. Why don't we bring it forward?

Nan All this week Yellow Jim's in Copenhagen doing a gig. (*Answering their puzzlement*) What they call a concert.

Bee Damnation.

Brigadier (*consulting his notes*) "Sleeping Beauty"'s not being danced again

Act I, Scene 2   25

until the twentieth. And "Centre Court" has to wait for the tennis championships.
Nan What about Hattie's other idea?
Hattie (*nervously*) What idea?
Nan Mrs Double-barrelled name.
Hattie Mrs Seymour Williams. (*Protesting*) But it was only a whiff of an idea.
Brigadier (*firing the question*) You said she was very wealthy?
Hattie Yes, rolling, but I——
Nan (*also attacking*) How did you think of persuading her?
Hattie I hadn't thought properly!
Brigadier You said something about dogs.
Hattie Yes, but I hadn't completely incorporated them.
Nan Tell us about them.
Hattie Oh, it's unfair! You're persecuting me!
Bee No, no, Hattie dear: just very interested in an idea that might save our bacon.
Hattie It won't! It could get us all frizzled.
Nan Tell us the facts, and see if we can't cook them up.
Hattie Well—Mrs Seymour Williams is very acquisitive. So I thought we wouldn't have too much trouble getting her here by pretending we had something she could add to her treasures——
Nan What sort of thing?
Hattie What she's most proud of is her collection of card-cases.
Brigadier Card-cases?
Bee I know. Those lovely flat cases we used to put our visiting cards in in the good old days.
Hattie (*nodding*) Some of them are evidently worth hundreds nowadays, and she'd go to Timbuctoo to get a rare one.
Brigadier Sounds promising. But when she arrives, and we haven't got anything?
Nan Easy. They belong to a friend who's bringing them round, and never arrives.
Brigadier Then how do we get her money?
Hattie I told you she's silly about dogs. Silly enough I think (*slowly*) to help me pay ransom if I arrive and say my little dog's been kidnapped.

They all look doubtful

Bee Well, I suppose she might.
Hattie (*urgently*) I know you were once bitten by one, Dame Beatrice. But for some people dogs take the place of children. Perhaps even love them more because they're dumb.
Nan (*pensively*) D'you know I'm not sure it's not rather a spiffing idea.
Hattie (*encouraged*) I'd pay up to save somebody's dog. And it's not cruel because there wouldn't be a real dog.
Bee (*thoughtfully*) It's very good in a way because we wouldn't have to cover our tracks at all.
Nan (*enthusiastically*) Let's try it! (*To Hattie*) Have you got her number?

Hattie (*nodding and taking out a notebook*) She lives just round the corner, but don't you think——
Brigadier Now, wait a minute, wait a minute——
Bee If we wait all the minutes you want, Bertie, we'll have the Middle East next door with strange smells and worse noises.
Brigadier God forbid!
Bee It's up to us, not him. Dial her, Hattie.
Hattie (*doing so*) I couldn't possibly speak! It'll be all I can do to carry out the second part.
Nan I don't mind talking to her. In fact would rather enjoy it. I shall be an Italian Countess.
Brigadier For God's sake why?
Nan I was very good as one in a play once.
Hattie (*gasping*) She's answering!
Nan (*taking the receiver*) Pronto? Signora Seymour Villiams? Ah, bon giorno, Signora. I am Contessa Francesca Ribolini. (*Listening and then repeating syllable by syllable*) Francesca Rosanna Ri-bo-li-ni.
Bee (*sotto voce*) Careful, Eleanor Duse!
Nan I shall sell soon my collection of card-cases. Is possibel you might like? . . . Variosa, Signora. Ma buonissima! . . . But naturentemente, Signora. I am this moment take them to my cara amica Dame Beatrice Appleby who also like.
Bee (*horrified*) I don't!
Nan Albert 'all Mansions, Signora: the portiere will direct you. But aspeto, Signora. I have to have part English cash because all my money is Italian lire. . . . Bene. Grazie. Grazie, Signora. Arriverderci, cara Signora. (*She puts down the phone*) She's on her way.
Hattie Oh, no!
Bee Dear Mother! You shouldn't have said I like them: I know absolutely nothing about card-cases.
Nan Then you're interested because you have an American friend who's asked you to find them for her. It's shaping beautifully. I shall be terribly grand, and appear totally disinterested in money.
Brigadier You don't appear at all: that's the point.
Nan Damn, neither I do. What a swizz.
Bee Hattie's the dog owner, what are you, Bertie? We want to impress her. Could you be the butler?
Brigadier No, I could not!
Nan You have all the clothes: from the bread-sauce party.
Bee (*hastily*) We agreed to forget that.
Nan I know! I'll be a French au pair girl instead.
Brigadier (*acidly*) The French part might pass: the rest certainly wouldn't.
Bee (*hastily*) Yes, I don't think that's exactly what's wanted.
Brigadier To stop even odder ideas I agree to be the butler.
Bee Splendid. One who's been with the family for years so that it won't look odd if you join in in emergency.
Hattie Emergency!

Act I, Scene 2   27

Bee Only a precaution. (*Pensively*) Another is to have someone to distract her if she asks questions we can't immediately answer.
Nan Shall I be a rich potty relation from Australia?
Hattie (*frantically*) No! She has a sister in Adelaide.
Nan Damnation.
Bee (*pensively*) Again someone who has a reason to join in.
Nan Got it! I'll be your companion. Then I'd know about everything.
Brigadier Good, Miss Parry. Now as soon as we've got the money, we have to get rid of her. How?
Nan The Countess rings up with a change of mind.
Brigadier That's it, splendid! Our old telephone routine. Once you've got the ransom, Miss Hatfield——
Hattie (*piteously*) Why did I ever think of this idea!
Brigadier —you beetle off to (*pointing out of window*) that phone-box in the park, and ring immediately you see the signal from this window.
Nan Yellow duster: immediate action. White duster: frantic emergency.
Hattie Don't! Mention that word again, and you'll have me flat on the floor.

The telephone rings. Hattie jumps

Could the gods be so good as to have changed her mind?
Nan (*starting to go to the phone*) Hope not now. (*Stopping*) No. If it's Mrs Seymour Williams she mustn't hear me: I wouldn't have had time to get here.
Bee If it's Mrs Spanager again I should be rude to her. You answer, Hattie.

Hattie goes reluctantly to the phone

If it's her say I'm drunk.
Hattie (*frantically*) You must give me something more likely.
Bee In the middle of making a cheese soufflé.
Hattie (*faintly into the phone*) Hullo?

There is a long silence while she listens with mounting horror

Brigadier What is it?
Hattie Just one moment. (*She covers the receiver*) It's Mr Andropolous! He's coming after all.
Bee He can't!
Brigadier We can't have one victim—(*correcting*)—one donor meeting another.
Bee Here give it to me. (*Into the phone*) Mr Andropolous? This is Dame Beatrice. I'm so awfully sorry, but I'm unexpectedly having to dash off to Kuala Lumpur.
Brigadier Don't ruin it for another time!
Bee But shall be flying back at the end of the week. And will ring you. Goodbye. (*She puts down the receiver*)
Brigadier Why Kuala Lumpur for God's sake?
Bee Can't think: I'm not even sure where it is.
Hattie I'm not sure where anything is. You must tell me. How do I know

when to come in with my beetle story? (*Frantically*) I don't mean my beetle story: my dog story.
Bee (*picking up the hand-bell*) I'll ring this when we've sort of softened her up. And if I ring it again, Bertie, it means we're in difficulties, and you must come in and help.
Brigadier Second bell, diversion needed. Understood. I'll go and tog up.

He hurries out

Hattie I suppose I'd look poor?
Bee Well, doggy, rather than poor.
Nan (*taking a shawl from a draped chair*) This shawl will do me. May I, Dame Beatrice?
Bee Certainly, if it doesn't disintegrate. I've had it since——

The telephone rings

Hattie Still hope! (*Into the phone*) Hullo? . . . Oh, thank you. (*She puts down the phone*) The porter says Mrs Seymour Williams is on her way up! (*Staggering slightly*) And I think I'm on my way down.
Nan Steady. There's nothing to be worried about.
Hattie There is!
Bee Now don't be silly, Hattie. Everything's going to be perfectly all right.
Hattie (*rushing and touching the table*) Oh! Don't tempt fate, Dame Beatrice.
Nan All our fates will be sealed if she comes in and finds you clinging to the table leg. (*She gives Hattie her coat, hat, scarf and apron*)
Hattie Oh yes. (*She starts to hurry out*) I come in when I hear the first bell?
Bee (*nodding*) And immediately you've finished, dash to the telephone box.
Hattie One day I'll dash away and you'll never see me again.

She flies out taking Nan's things with her

Nan (*ominously*) I hope you weren't a little optimistic saying everything'd go all right——

The front doorbell rings

Bee We shall soon know: there she is.

The Brigadier comes in. He has put on a wing-collar and old tail-coat, and wears ancient half-moon spectacles. He stoops, shuffles slightly and speaks very slowly

Brigadier Are you in to callers, madam?
Bee Wonderful, Bertie. You might have been doing it for years.
Brigadier (*cupping his ear*) I beg your pardon, madam?

The doorbell rings again

Nan That was the bell, Livingston.
Brigadier (*in his ordinary voice*) No, no, Livingston smacks too much of the Nile. James, I think.

The doorbell rings again

Act I, Scene 2   29

Bee (*impatiently*) All right, James. But go and open the door!
Brigadier (*going to the front door*) Very well, madam ... (*He opens the front door*) Good-afternoon, madam. Madam is expecting Madam. Mrs Seymour Williams, madam.

He shows in Mrs Seymour Williams, an elderly stern-looking woman, very expensively dressed, and with a forthright manner

Bee (*holding out her hand*) How nice of you to come, Mrs Seymour Williams.
Mrs Seymour Williams Only barbed wire could have kept me away.
Bee (*gesturing to Nan*) My companion, Lucy.
Mrs Seymour Williams How d'you do.
Nan (*suddenly rather gentle and ingratiating*) It's an honour to meet someone who I hear is such a connoisseur of the arts.
Mrs Seymour Williams Oh, I'm not at all. Merely an avid collector of small things.
Nan Oh, lucky you. I, alas, have never had a penny. And of course always living in other people's houses means that——
Bee (*interrupting warningly*) That you're a little inclined to talk too much, Lucy dear. Do sit down, Mrs Seymour Williams.
Mrs Seymour Williams (*doing so*) The Countess hasn't arrived?
Bee Not yet. Inform me when she does, James.
Brigadier I beg your pardon, madam?
Bee (*loudly*) I told you: I'm expecting the Countess Ribolini.
Brigadier I'll never be able to pronounce that mouthful ...

He goes out

Bee I'm afraid he's a little beyond it. But they are so difficult to get.
Mrs Seymour Williams Just how I feel. My old Mary's a complete fool, but she adores my dogs almost as much as I do, and would I ever get another? (*Conspiratorially*) Tell me quickly before the Countess arrives: are the card-cases as good as she says?
Bee (*after a moment's thought*) Better.
Mrs Seymour Williams Excellent. I've just rearranged my collection — turned out all the ordinary tortoiseshell and mother-of-pearl — so am just itching to replace with a few specials. (*After a moment*) I don't want to seem indiscreet, but does her bringing them here mean you are going to choose the best?
Bee I don't collect. I'm merely the go-between for an American dealer.
Mrs Seymour Williams (*grimly*) A dealer. Oh, I'm not pleased to hear that. I don't like dealers. And I hate haggling. I'd much rather pay over the odds than haggle. Does he have to see them?
Bee I beg your pardon?
Mrs Seymour Williams (*fiddling in her bag*) I'd rather any extra profit went to a good cause than a dealer. Have you a favourite charity?
Bee I have a — housing scheme for aged people I'm rather interested in.
Mrs Seymour Williams (*slipping a note into an envelope*) Be so good as to pass this on to them, will you?

Bee (*with a bland smile*) Such kindness has made me completely forget the dealer's name.
Mrs Seymour Williams Good. I'll leave it here. (*She lifts the hand-bell to put the envelope underneath it*)
Bee (*horrified*) Be careful! I mean — be careful the brass doesn't dirty your glove.

But the door flies open and Hattie hurries in

Hattie Oh, Dame Beatrice, Dame Beatrice, something terrible——
Bee No, no, it's a mistake. (*Trying to bustle her out*) I mean I'm sure you're mistaken, and that it's not really so terrible. Anyhow James will see to it for you——
Hattie Who?
Bee James.
Hattie James?
Bee (*firmly*) Yes James. He'll put it right for you. Off you go to him.

The bewildered Hattie is pushed out of the door

(*Closing the door*) I'm sorry, Mrs Seymour Williams. Our neighbour's a little — (*She makes a gesture towards her head*)
Mrs Seymour Williams Have you any idea the price the Countess has in mind?
Bee (*at a loss*) Uum — Lucy's really her friend; she'll have more idea.

Mrs Seymour Williams looks questioningly at Nan. Nan looks blank for a moment, then suddenly starts singing

Nan "Vissi d'arte, vissi d'amore — "
Bee Lucy, what are you doing?
Nan *Tosca*. One of Verdi's most lovely arias.
Bee But we're talking about card-cases not Verdi.
Nan Oh, I'm so sorry. It just came out. When one's only a paid employee — a poorly paid employee——
Bee (*firmly*) The price of the card-cases, Lucy.
Nan Millions.
Bee (*warningly*) It's very dangerous to exaggerate like that, Lucy.
Nan But I'm talking in lire, Dame Beatrice. And as there are — a great many to the pound, a million is nothing like it sounds.
Mrs Seymour Williams It still sounds a great deal. I hope I've brought enough: she said she wanted part in cash. But if it's in excess of a thousand pounds or so——

Bee gasps. Mrs Seymour Williams looks sharply at her

Nan (*quickly*) You poor dear, are you starting another attack of asthma? Shall I give you an injection?
Bee I think I can control it.
Mrs Seymour Williams I hope she's not going to be too long. I have another collection to see this afternoon, and may find all I want there.

Act I, Scene 2

Bee (*after a moment's thought*) If I could do anything — (*doing so*) like ringing this little bell, to hurry her, I would.

The Brigadier comes in

Brigadier Yes, madam?
Bee (*upset at seeing him instead of Hattie*) Yes, what?
Brigadier You wanted me, madam?
Bee No, not you.
Brigadier But I thought I heard the bell, madam.
Bee You did.
Brigadier (*puzzled*) But you did not want me, madam?
Bee No.

Mrs Seymour Williams looks at her

(*Seeing this*) I wanted Cook.
Brigadier Cook?
Bee (*impatiently*) Yes, Cook. You know who she is. Tell her I want the partridges broiled tonight.
Brigadier (*at a complete loss*) Ah!
Bee Did you hear what I said?
Brigadier Cook. Broiled.
Bee Yes.
Brigadier Ah.
Bee Well, go and tell her.
Brigadier (*going*) Very well, madam.
Bee With mushroom sauce.
Brigadier With mushroom sauce — ah . . .

He goes out mystified

Bee I always like mushroom sauce with partridge, don't you?
Mrs Seymour Williams I regret to say I've very little interest in food.
Bee Oh, what you miss. (*After a worried pause*) Did you notice the tone of this little bell? (*Ringing it*) So clear for such a small bell.

Hattie dashes in

Hattie Is it all right for me to come in?
Bee Yes! I mean, hasn't James put your trouble right?
Hattie (*meaningly*) No. He's completely at a loss.
Bee He'll come to eventually. (*To Mrs Seymour Williams*) You don't mind, as the Countess has obviously been held up in the traffic?

Mrs Seymour Williams waves permission

Tell us, what is it?
Hattie It's terrible, quite terrible . . .
Nan We have gathered that, dear. But what is?
Hattie Timothy. They've got him.
Bee What do you mean, "got him"?

Hattie Seized him. Kidnapped him.
Mrs Seymour Williams Your little boy?
Nan Her little dog, only he's big.
Hattie We were walking along in the park as happy as Larry one moment, and then the next, two men appeared from nowhere, scooped him up and were gone before I realized what was happening.
Bee My dear!
Nan How quite dreadful.
Mrs Seymour Williams You should have gone straight to the police.
Hattie Yes, I should, shouldn't I? (*Inspired*) But you see, I couldn't! They left a note on the grass saying Timothy would suffer if I did, but they'd contact me.
Bee And have they?
Hattie (*frantically*) That's what I've been trying to tell you. They're on the phone now. Demanding money. I told them it was no good – that I was only a penniless swimming-instructress. But they just got nastier.
Mrs Seymour Williams (*rising*) Leave it to me; I know what to do. I'm a Justice of the Peace.
Bee (*really alarmed*) What!
Mrs Seymour Williams A magistrate. Used to dealing with these sort of people. Where's the phone?
Bee Now wait a moment——
Mrs Seymour Williams Certainly not; we must act immediately.

They watch in horror as she goes to the phone

Nan No, no, don't phone, please——
Mrs Seymour Williams Why not?
Hattie (*stepping into the breach*) I've told you why not. They said I wasn't to inform anyone. That if I did – oh, it's too terrible – that if I did, they'd cut off his tail.
Bee No! Not that lovely big fluffy tail?
Hattie Yes! (*To Mrs Seymour Williams*) It's his pride and joy. And mine. I can't tell you what it looks like after it's been shampooed. A great waving glory. Without it – oh, I can't bear to think of it.
Nan No, of course you can't. How much do they want?

Hattie looks completely blank

Hundreds perhaps?
Hattie Yes, hundreds.
Bee (*to Mrs Seymour Williams*) The poor thing's in shock. How many hundreds, dear?
Hattie (*after a frantic think*) Five.
Mrs Seymour Williams Five hundred pounds?
Hattie (*nodding*) In unmarked notes.
Bee But nobody has money like that just lying about.
Hattie Oh, please! If I don't produce it immediately they said – oh – it's too dreadful – they said they'd post me his ear.
Mrs Seymour Williams How abominable.

Act I, Scene 2   33

Hattie (*wailing*) I couldn't bear it — I couldn't bear it!
Nan No, of course you couldn't, you poor dear. (*To the others*) Five hundred pounds in cash. I'm only a poorly paid employee, but there must be something somebody can do.
Mrs Seymour Williams There is: get on to Scotland Yard. (*Going to the phone*) They'll be round in a flash if they know I'm concerned.
Bee No. It'd put the dog in danger.
Hattie Please help in some other way, please.
Nan (*to Mrs Seymour Williams*) Dear lady, do I remember you saying you had a certain amount of cash in your bag?
Bee Of course! I know it's a lot to ask but do you think you could possibly——
Mrs Seymour Williams (*firmly*) No, I do not.
Hattie Oh, couldn't you? You'd know what I was going through if you had a dog of your own.
Mrs Seymour Williams I have; two of the most adorable.
Hattie Then imagine what they'd look like without their tails.
Mrs Seymour Williams Don't suggest something so awful.
Hattie (*pressing her advantage*) Or even worse: think of four ears on your breakfast tray.
Mrs Seymour Williams Too horrible to imagine.
Hattie Then you'll——
Mrs Seymour Williams Do what we should have done right at the beginning. (*Going to the phone again*) Summon the police.
Bee No, wait a minute——
Mrs Seymour Williams Certainly not. (*Thumbing through her address book*) Such men must be caught, and brought to court. With as much publicity as possible so that it'll deter any other such fiends. Where's that damn number?
Bee I really don't want the police here.
Mrs Seymour Williams Rubbish. It's our duty as responsible citizens. Let alone mine as a representative of the law. (*She starts dialling*)
Hattie This is ghastly!
Nan (*urgently*) We must do something!
Bee (*frantically ringing the bell*) Perhaps James can help.
Mrs Seymour Williams (*to Hattie*) What's your number so that they can tap the line till the flying squad arrives?

The Brigadier comes in

Brigadier You wanted me, madam?
Bee Yes, do something.
Brigadier Yes, madam. What? Ring the police?
Mrs Seymour Williams (*into the phone*) Hullo?

Nan sings "Vissi d'arte, vissi d'amore" loudly near her

Quiet, please! (*Into the phone*) Inspector Ashton. Immediately. Urgent.
Nan No! Stop! Stop! It's all right. It's all right.
Mrs Seymour Williams How can it be?

Nan (*pointing out of the window*) There he is. The dog. The one with the great fluffy tail. (*Almost dragging Hattie to the window*) That's him, isn't it?
Hattie (*not understanding*) Where? Where?
Nan There! Near that lamp-post.
Bee Yes! That's him; I'd know him anywhere.
Mrs Seymour Williams (*laying down the receiver*) Where?
Nan Just going through that door. Oh, you've missed him.
Bee He must have escaped and rushed home. How wonderful.
Hattie Oh, yes. Really wonderful. To think it's all over.
Bee (*urgently*) It isn't till you've rushed to let him in.
Hattie Oh yes, of course I must. I'm a bit bewildered. Bewildered but relieved. So relieved I'm going to burst into tears ...

She does so and rushes out whimpering

As she does, Nan nips to the phone and replaces the receiver

Nan Also a great relief we shan't have the men in blue tramping all over the place.
Mrs Seymour Williams Of course we must still contact them.
Bee (*firmly*) I shall. I shall report the whole matter to my nephew, who is a commissioner. But thank you very much for all your help.
Brigadier You won't be wanting me then, madam?
Bee No, James. At least — perhaps Mrs Seymour Williams would like you to show her to the lift. (*To Mrs Seymour Williams*) As something has obviously happened to delay the Countess I'm sure you'd prefer to leave.
Mrs Seymour Williams Certainly not. (*Sitting*) I've wasted so much time that I'm determined it shall be fruitful in the end.

They gaze at her in alarm. She looks sharply back at them

Nan (*singing*) "Vissi d'arte, vissi d'amore"
Bee You'd better bring in some sherry, James.
Brigadier There isn't — I mean Cook has just used the last bottle in tonight's trifle.
Mrs Seymour Williams I don't drink midday anyhow, thank you.

There is a pause. Nan starts singing again

Bee Oh, do stop that, Lucy.
Nan I'm so sorry: it keeps going round in my head.
Bee Well, leave it there.

Another pause

Mrs Seymour Williams I really am beginning to get a little impatient. Couldn't you ring this woman and make sure there's been no misunderstanding?
Bee (*doubtfully*) Yes, yes. I could do that ...

The Brigadier takes a yellow duster from his pocket and hurries to the window

Brigadier Blighters! I see I've missed one or two of their webs. (*He waves the duster while pretending to remove them*)

Act I, Scene 2   35

Mrs Seymour Williams Must he do that now?
Bee He doesn't quite realize what's going on.
Mrs Seymour Williams (*annoyed*) Well, give me the Countess's number and I'll phone her myself.
Nan That's not the way to deal with spiders. Have you a clean duster?
Brigadier I think so, Miss Lucy. (*Immediately he hands her a white duster*)
Nan (*waving it frantically*) Down, you little devils, down.
Mrs Seymour Williams Dame Beatrice, I really must insist——

The telephone rings

Bee Thank goodness! (*Recovering*) Probably the porter to say she's on her way up. Answer please, Lucy.
Nan (*hurrying to the phone*) As usual: your wish is my command. (*She lifts the receiver*) Yes? (*Pretending to listen*) Yes. No! Yes. No! No!!
Bee Come along, come along, what is it?
Nan (*on the phone*) Yes. Of course. Goodbye. (*She puts down the receiver*) Bad news, I fear.
Bee What?
Nan The Countess Ribolini has had a serious fall.
Mrs Seymour Williams Oh no!
Bee But how terrible.
Nan Blood, hysterics, hospital. The lot. And that red hair is a wig: it fell off.
Bee Oh, the poor darling. It's calamitous. And poor you, Mrs Seymour Williams, having waited all this time.
Mrs Seymour Williams It's quite awful. I'd made up my mind to have her cases.
Bee I am so sorry. But there's absolutely nothing we can do. And I'm afraid you'll have to excuse us: we must rush to the hospital.
Mrs Seymour Williams Now, wait a minute, wait a minute. I'm not going to let them slip through my hands so easily. (*Taking out her note-book*) Her full address and telephone number, please.

Behind her back Bee gazes frantically at the Brigadier. He snatches up both dusters again and waves them frantically

Brigadier There they are again: I think they must be breeding.
Bee (*to Mrs Seymour Williams*) He has an absolute mania about them.
Mrs Seymour Williams I can see. I shall write to her. And her solicitor in case she succumbs. First her full name and title?

When Bee doesn't answer she looks up sharply

Bee I'm so sorry: I was worrying about the spiders. Umm——

She is saved by the telephone ringing

  It may be the hospital again. Quickly, Lucy. (*Anxiously*) Do you know what to say?
Nan I think I have an idea. (*Into the phone*) Yes? (*Pretending to listen*) Who? What name? (*Listening and looking at Mrs Seymour Williams*) Oh yes, yes, she's here.

Mrs Seymour Williams Me?
Nan Yes, I can. (*She listens*) No! (*Each one more urgent*) No! No!!
Mrs Seymour Williams What is it? What is it?
Nan (*on the phone*) I'll tell her straight away. Don't take any action. She'll probably dash back. Goodbye. (*She puts down phone*) You must be brave, my poor Mrs Seymour Williams.
Mrs Seymour Williams Why? What? What?
Nan It was your Mary. Says two men are at the door saying they're dog-walkers and have instructions to take your two for walkies.
Mrs Seymour Williams (*immediately agitated*) But they haven't! They can't possibly! It's a trick.
Brigadier Probably those dog-snatchers again, madam.
Mrs Seymour Williams My darling Shoo-Shoo and Jee-Jee. I'd die if anything happened to them.
Nan No need to panic. I told her not to let them go till you got back.
Mrs Seymour Williams But I must clear up this business here first.
Bee (*urgently*) No, no. Those crooks first. It's your duty as a citizen. Let alone as a magistrate.
Mrs Seymour Williams But those card-cases are so important to me.
Nan (*forcefully*) Those men must be caught, and brought to court.
Mrs Seymour Williams Yes, you're right. What are the cases compared to my dogs? I must get back immediately. Ring and say I'm on my way. But do nothing till I arrive. And warn the police. Oh, it's all too awful. All that waiting, no cases, the snatches, the spiders: a ghastly afternoon, thank you so much . . .

She hurries out overseen by the Brigadier

Bee (*sinking into a chair*) Yes, a truly ghastly afternoon.
Nan (*also sinking down*) I feel like a very old carpet that's been hoovered too much. Though I have to say: I did enjoy one or two bits of it.
Bee Rather too much.
Nan Oh dear, d'you think so. Once started I do get rather carried away.
Bee (*worriedly*) Bertie's going to be furious. Get ready for a hail of "told-you-sos".
Nan Suppose we play it very apologetic and contrite? Might that be the best way to weather the storm?
Bee Oh, just let it blow itself out, I think.

The Brigadier comes in carrying a tray and glasses

Brigadier (*still as the butler*) After such a hectic time I thought Madam and Miss Lucy might like a little encouragement from my own private bottle.
Bee (*surprised*) Oh, that's very kind of you, Bertie.
Nan Most kind.
Brigadier (*back to normal*) Well, you did extremely well.
Bee (*staggered*) You think so?
Brigadier Considering the appalling mess we'd got ourselves in, you got us out miraculously.
Bee But when she gets back and finds there've been no dog-snatchers?

Act I, Scene 2   37

Nan (*blandly*) Someone's sick joke that fortunately had no ill effects.
Bee But those damn card-cases: she won't let them drop.
Nan Quite awful, but while the Countess was in hospital they were stolen.

Hattie comes in limply

Hattie Oh, dear, I'm so sorry I was such a failure.
Brigadier You battled through with decided courage considering the onslaught.
Hattie (*cheering up*) Oh, thank you. I saw your signal straight away, but men kept banging on the window and in my embarrassment I dropped the coins on the floor.
Brigadier We all had our weaknesses. Have some whisky.
Hattie Now?!
Brigadier Well, there certainly won't be any left tomorrow.
Hattie Oh, thank you, then.
Brigadier Here's to our at least having completed the mission.

They murmur and drink

That it was an almost total failure is not, perhaps, quite such a serious setback as it might seem at first consideration.

They all look surprised

Nan Oh?
Bee Really?
Hattie Isn't it?
Brigadier We were inclined to be far too optimistic, and to underestimate the enormous difficulties these sort of missions involve. This near-fiasco has pin-pointed the extreme dangers, and the urgent need for far greater planning, preparation, training and discipline.
Nan You're absolutely right, Brigadier.
Hattie Nobody can appreciate it more than me.
Bee Indeed. And I must say I think it very noble of you to take it in this spirit.
Nan Here, here.
Hattie Most relieving.
Brigadier Thank you. (*Enjoying their attention*) I do so partly because I realized that morale would be at rock-bottom; and mustn't stay there. But far more importantly that the ideas and improvisations and — I must use the word — sheer "guts" that you all showed in the shadow of disaster, means that we're perfectly capable of triumph.
Hattie I do hope you're right.
Nan Of course we are.
Bee Bravo, Bertie.
Brigadier So let us regard this morning not as a failure, but as a case of *reculer pour mieux sauter*.

Hattie gasps

Which I can see Miss Hatfield fully understands as meaning taking a step backwards the better to leap forward again.

Hattie Oh, yes, yes.

Nan That's the spirit, Brigadier.

Bee Beautifully put.

Brigadier So I ask you to raise your glasses, ladies, to the certain successes we must, and shall, have in the very near future.

Bee To inspiration, and the strength to carry it out.

Nan To speedy triumph.

Hattie To end of frights. (*Lowering her glass*) Though even after that delicious sip, I don't quite see how we proceed.

Brigadier (*energetically*) By banishing such pessimism, and starting, immediately, to re-think, re-plan, and re-organize. (*Clapping his hands*) So come along: gather round in a circle, and concentrate enormously.

They stand, at attention, round him

Now: bearing in mind the vital necessity of securing the annexe at all costs, we must launch a series of full-frontal attacks——

Hattie sinks to the floor with a whimper

Nan The poor beast's fainted.

Brigadier (*mercilessly*) Prop her up and continue listening. (*Commandingly*) We must support these assaults with remorseless diversional skirmishes on the enemy's flanks—and heedless of casualties——

The CURTAIN *and a long moan from Hattie cut him off in full spate*

ACT II

The same. Two months later. Afternoon

The walls are hung with dust-sheets, and the furniture pushed against them, except for the desk and table: the former with neat piles of papers and a typewriter; the other covered with green baize, and a bowl of flowers. The first has an expensively printed notice: "MISS MURIEL MORTIMER", the other: "CRUISE MANAGER". Pinned on the sheets are large glossy travel posters and a map of the world

The telephone rings

Bee comes in, carrying an enormous potted palm. She places it, and goes to the phone

Bee Hullo? ... Yes, Mr Baines. ... No, Mr Baines. ... Well, tell Mrs Spanager's solicitor to boil his head and play with the fat. ... Listen, Mr Baines: I'm paying you to hold up the signing of the contract till we have the full amount—which will be soon. If you can't think up a few little stumbling blocks, I certainly shall when it comes to settling your bill. ... Well, have a small fire! ... Then send me the contract and I'll have a small fire.

As she listens the Brigadier comes in with another potted palm

Yes, do that, Mr Baines. And don't ring with any more silliness or you'll have a defamation of character case on your hands. Goodbye. (*She puts down the phone*) Old idiot! I've paid him a fortune over the years, and yet——(*breaking off*). I wonder if we might get some of it back! What about an "Operation Lincoln's Inn Fields"?

Brigadier I think it wiser to keep our distance from the law.

Bee It would have a double satisfaction though; I shall bring it up at the next planning session. Perhaps that one matching mine but on the other side?

The Brigadier places the palm

Splendid. It looks marvellously imposing and officey.

Hattie comes in walking awkwardly

Hattie I've got it!
Brigadier (*crossly*) But you weren't supposed to get it till next Wednesday, Miss Hatfield.
Hattie I know. But my family unexpectedly went off to the zoo for the day. So I thought I'd better strike while the iron was hot.

Brigadier (*impatiently*) Well, let's have a look.
Hattie All right. There! (*She undoes her coat revealing a carpet wrapped round her*)
Bee Well done! Most brave.
Brigadier Let's hope you'll get it back as easily after the operation.
Hattie They'll be skiing: it'll be a snip. (*Seeing the notice*) Oh, lovely! "Muriel Mortimer." I wish it wasn't only for the afternoon; I'd much rather be a secretary than a cleaning lady.
Bee (*wistfully*) I'd much rather be a housekeeper at the *Berkeley Hotel*. I had a lovely time. And was paid far too much.
Brigadier I should hope so after those superlative references I wrote you.
Bee But if you hadn't made me leave I'd have been able to afford a lovely new pair of Italian shoes.
Brigadier Once you'd found this American it wasn't safe to stay: she might have recognized you.
Bee The housekeeper's never seen by the guests. I got the maid who looks after her suite to leak all the details.
Brigadier It was an avoidable risk.
Bee (*sighing*) I suppose you're right, Bertie.
Brigadier We have enough unavoidable ones. (*Looking at a clip-board*) I'm not happy about this afternoon's two operations following each other so quickly.
Hattie I hope my nerves stand up to two in one day.
Bee They've been timed and planned, and retimed and replanned till we could do them hanging upside down.
Hattie There always seem to be bits which go differently from the plans.
Brigadier (*dangerously*) So what do you suggest?
Hattie (*quickly*) Oh, nothing, nothing! I'm not complaining, just worrying.
Brigadier Quite unnecessarily. (*Looking at his watch*) But perhaps you'd better go and get ready: there's just a possibility Mrs Mayer will be here early. Nan's left to fetch her from the *Berkeley*, but if traffic's light Mr Ashmore can only drive her round a certain amount or she may spot a landmark.
Bee From what I saw of her she's so dizzy she wouldn't be able to find this flat again if we gave her a marked map.
Brigadier We can't be too careful.
Hattie Oh, you're so right, Brigadier! (*Collecting the carpet*) Shall we put this down as further window-dressing?
Brigadier Something might happen to it. Far safer hidden in your room till we use it.
Hattie (*going*) All right. I'll put it in the hollow bit on top of the wardrobe. Won't be long — I've laid out my clothes ready.

She goes out

Brigadier (*annoyed*) I do wish she'd keep to plans! She'll make another awful mistake if she's not careful.
Bee She was wonderful in "Operation Mayfair Hairdresser".
Brigadier Yes, but "Operation Centre Court" was going perfectly, too, till she lost her head.

Act II   41

Bee It was our fault for not warning her about present-day tennis stars. Even I'd have been upset if he'd called me what he called her.
Brigadier But you wouldn't have rushed from the restaurant screaming.
Bee No, I'd have finished my Lobster Thermidor first. (*Savouring the memory*) It was a delicious meal, wasn't it?
Brigadier Those oysters! Yes, at least we got that out of "Operation Centre Court".

The telephone rings

Bee (*going to it*) That raspberry soufflé! (*She kisses the tips of her fingers and picks up the phone*) Hullo? Oh, thank you. (*She puts down the phone*) Hall porter. Nan and Mrs Mayer have just come through from the back-entrance.
Brigadier Ah! (*Going to the door and calling*) Miss Hatfield. Positions.
Bee (*sitting at the Director's desk (the table) and placing a fur stole round her shoulders*) I borrowed this from my doctor's wife: you don't think it's going too far?
Brigadier Not for such an extremely exclusive travel agency. Which reminds me — (*fishing about in his pocket*) — I have a tie-pin here I want you to consider. (*Fixing it into his tie*) From a pre-war Christmas cracker, but she'll never know.
Bee Most imposing. And why not a buttonhole? (*She takes a carnation from the vase and fixes it for him*) Yes, you look the part perfectly.

Hattie hurries in with a pad and pencil. She looks quite smart in a plain dress, her hair pulled behind her ears, and upswept glasses

Hattie Are you ready to dictate, Madam Director?
Bee Splendid, Hattie.
Hattie (*going and sitting at her desk*) Shall I be typing when she comes in?
Bee No, better if it's quiet so that she immediately concentrates on — (*nodding towards the Brigadier*) — the bait.
Brigadier (*jumping up*) The firm's notice! (*He picks up an expensively printed notice "TRAVEL. BY APPOINTMENT ONLY" and hurrying to the front door hangs it up outside*)
Bee (*to Hattie*) But tap loudly if anything seems to be going awkwardly.
Brigadier (*hurrying back, and sitting in the chair in front of Bee's desk*) Think I heard their voices. Now, remember: once we've got her "contribution", all concentrate on getting rid of her: we're sunk if she overshoots the next victim.
Bee (*correcting*) Donor.

There is a warning ring on the front doorbell and Nan — smart in a blue suit and yachting cap — ushers in Mrs Maxine Mayer, who is a pretty, late middle-aged woman, well-dressed by American standards. She talks quickly, with a Southern American accent, and laughs in a tinkling way

(*pretending not to see them*) I rather feel that even with a de-luxe state-cabin you'd find the cruise a little long, My Lord.
Nan Mrs Maxine Mayer, Madame Director.
Bee (*rising*) Oh, Mrs Mayer, I do apologize. We're slightly behind schedule.

Will you forgive me if I ask you to wait a moment while I finish with Lord Radnage? He has to get back to the House of Lords.
Maxine Sure, sure, sure, honey. (*Hurrying to curl exaggeratedly on the sofa*) I'll be a mouse. A humble, awed, but very impressed little mouse.
Nan Can I get you a drink, madam?
Maxine (*in an exaggerated whisper*) It's kind, honey, but why do I need a drink when I can swallow down the words of the lord?
Nan Then if you'll excuse me, Madam Director, I'll just check your query about the best time to see elephant seals in Guadaloupe.

She goes out

Bee Now, My Lord. The following morning you arrive at Belém, in Brazil. Where you could visit the native market, and perhaps buy at the medicine stalls which sell potions made out of snakes' skins, skunks' tails and lizards' tongues.
Brigadier Unnecessary, if my valet remembers to pack Epsom salts, tincture of iodine, and aspirin tablets.

Maxine tinkles

Maxine I apologize, I really do. But how can I be a mouse when he's so witty?
Bee The following day, on the river itself, you will hear howler monkeys from the forest.
Hattie And don't forget the raucous cries of the colourful parrots as they fly from one bank to the other, Madam Director.
Bee Thank you, Miss Mortimer. (*To the Brigadier*) We have all, of course, experienced the cruises, so that we can advise from personal knowledge.
Brigadier But you can't completely recommend this cruise one hundred percent?
Bee (*doubtfully*) Well, it's very luxurious, and the ship's beautiful——
Hattie When it was refurbished they used eight thousand yards of lime-green carpet.
Bee (*coldly*) Thank you, Miss Mortimer! (*Graciously to the Brigadier again*) But to my mind it wouldn't begin to compare with (*lowering her voice, and glancing at Mrs Mayer*) what I may only refer to as: Cruise X.
Brigadier Then after so many years complete satisfaction with your firm, I shall take your advice. Book me the best cabin you can obtain on Cruise X.
Bee Thank you, My Lord. (*She makes a note*) You do fully realize why much as I dislike it—we are obliged to ask a large deposit in cash?
Brigadier (*producing an envelope*) The circumstances being so very unusual, it's perfectly reasonable. Here is the full fifteen percent, plus a few odd pounds to buy flowers for the office.
Bee How kind.
Hattie A typical gesture from our most favourite client: thank you, My Lord.
Bee Then if you'll be so good as to wait while Miss Mortimer makes out a few papers——

The Brigadier rises

Unless his presence would inconvenience you, Mrs Mayer?

Act II

Maxine What'd inconvenience me would be if he left before I saw the front of him. I've only seen the back so far. And though it's the most lovely straight back I've seen even in England——
Bee I'm sorry—let me introduce you. Mrs Mayer, Lord Radnage.
Maxine (*shaking hands*) I'm sure I ought to curtsy or something. But if I did we'd probably both end on the carpet. And though that'd be lovely for me, I feel you other girls might knife me.
Brigadier It's a privilege to meet such a charming representative of your country, Mrs Mayer.
Maxine Call me Maxine, and my cup is full.
Brigadier Of course, Maxine.
Maxine (*tinkling*) It's not full, it's slopping in the saucer.
Bee If you'll be so kind as to sit here, Mrs Mayer? I do apologize for the appalling state of this room, but as you see we're in the middle of redecoration.
Maxine But I love it, honey: reminds me of a hotel I stayed at in Delhi, India.
Bee I'm afraid I wasn't absolutely certain on the phone exactly why you wanted to come to see me, Mrs Mayer?
Maxine It was my sweet little maid at the *Berkeley*. When she saw all the stickers on my luggage and heard what a sucker for travel I am, she said I must come to you, or might miss the "experience of my life"! And arranged it all before I'd even put on my stockings. So here I am. (*With a glance at the Brigadier*) And am I glad I am!
Bee Well, I very much fear there's been a little indiscretion somewhere. We only deal with clients such as Lord Radnage, who are either well known to us, or very personally recommended.
Maxine You make me feel sea-sick!
Brigadier I think, if I may say so, that I'm a fair judge of character. And that you'd be perfectly safe with Maxine.
Maxine Oh, isn't that dear of you! You're not only beautiful, you're sweet. (*Not making the point too strongly*) I hope your wife appreciates you.
Brigadier My wife fell off the perch years ago.
Maxine As did my last hubby. What a bond, eh?

She tinkles. Hattie types furiously

So am I accepted?
Bee I, of course, bow to his lordship. But you'll have to promise, by all you hold sacred——
Maxine (*holding her rosary*) My rosary I got blessed by the Pope himself in Rome, Italy.
Bee To keep the details of a cruise I shall tell you about a complete and absolute secret. (*Emphasizing*) To be revealed to no-one whatsoever.
Maxine If I breathe a word may I grow to look like one of those women in Papua New Guinea.
Bee Then I have to tell you your maid was right. This is an opportunity that'll be offered to very few. But I must warn you will be extremely expensive.
Maxine Have no worries there, honey. My first was in refrigeration, my second in plastics. I've got it. In plenty.

Bee It's a chance quite beyond the grasp of even the most privileged tourist.
Maxine I feel as excited as when I saw my first elephant in Kenya, Africa.
Bee (*lowering her voice*) As you may, or may not know, our Royal Family — our most treasured institution——
Hattie God bless them.
Bee (*silencing her with a glance*) — are not properly supported by the State. The sovereign has actually to make up the short fall from her own private purse——
Brigadier Disgraceful! As I've said on many an occasion in the House.
Bee Obviously only a certain amount of economy can be undertaken without threatening the dignity of the Crown. So, another solution was sought. And someone — I am not revealing which of them — came up with the idea of Cruise X.
Maxine You can't mean——?
Bee (*nodding gravely*) A few very privileged persons are going to be allowed to join the next cruise of the Royal Yacht *Britannia*.
Maxine (*dramatically*) I feel the same as when we were about to shoot the rapids on the Amazon. (*Opening her eyes again*) You mean, with — "them"?
Bee Certain members of the Royal Family will surely be there. But you must appreciate that this is a cruise where there can be no stated schedules or sailing dates.
Maxine (*excitedly*) Sure, sure. I don't mind when we go, how we go, where we go. Just let me go!
Bee That, I'm afraid, is not entirely in our hands, Mrs Mayer. Nothing can be done till I have forwarded your name to the Palace. They will make their own enquiries.
Maxine (*in despair*) They'll never accept me! My "third" made his money in china bathroom fittings — (*closing her eyes*) including the ones you sit on.
Brigadier It is *you* who are going on the cruise, Maxine. As I shall remind Her Majesty's Private Secretary.
Maxine I don't know what the next step up from a lord is, but you should be it! And have a more exciting voice than even that boys' choir I heard in Vienna, Austria. (*To Bee*) So what do I have to do?
Bee There's the slight question of finance. (*Passing her a paper*) I've jotted down the approximate cost.
Maxine (*looking*) Alleluia! That's more than I paid when I went one and a half times round the world.
Bee (*severely*) If I may say so any comparison is almost lese-majesty.
Maxine (*hastily*) Oh, yes, yes, yes, I'm not bellyaching. (*Scuffling about in her handbag*) Just fussed I may not have brought enough travellers' cheques for the deposit. The girl said you wanted cash, but I imagined the whole amount would only add up to peanuts. (*Very worried*) I've only got five thousand dollars.
Bee (*involuntarily*) Five thousand!
Maxine (*anxiously*) Not enough?
Bee (*recovering*) Well, I suppose it's a gesture. And as you have such a sweet honest face: just sign them, will you? (*To Hattie*) See Madam is sent a receipt for this little amount first thing in the morning. Miss Mortimer.

Act II   45

Hattie You don't have to tell me such a routine matter, Madam Director; it's automatic.
Bee (*rising*) Then — (*tinkling the handbell*) — there is no more we can do till we hear from Buckingham Palace.
Maxine There's more I can do! I can take you all back to the *Berkeley*, and we'll open the biggest bottle of bubbly they've got. Come on.

Hattie taps furiously

Nan comes in

Nan You rang, madam?
Bee Take Mrs Mayer back to the *Berkeley*, please, Miss Arbuthnot.
Nan Actually I have the Baron on the line about his trip to Santa Cruz, madam.
Bee (*slightly taken aback*) Mrs Mayer is more important than any foreign baron, Miss Arbuthnot. Escort her first, please.
Nan Of course, madam.
Maxine (*to Nan*) You must come and wallow in bubbly as well, honey.
Bee Mightn't it be a little unwise to tempt providence until after you're accepted?
Maxine I see why the Royals give you their business. But once you've got their OK we'll swim in the stuff. That includes you, of course, Your Lordship.
Brigadier I fear I have too many laws to help draft. But there'll be plenty of time to celebrate on board.
Maxine You mean you'll be there as well as "them"?!
Bee Lord Radnage will be accepted automatically, of course.
Maxine The Royals plus a suave and unattached pillar of the aristocracy! My feet no longer touch the floor. (*To Nan*) Give me your arm, honey, and guide my floating. (*To Bee*) I'll be waiting at the end of the phone like a hooked salmon. But if the strain's too much I'll tinkle you: I've copied the number off the phone there. Have a good life everyone!

She goes out followed by Nan

The others are all appalled

But as they are about to speak Nan comes back, and hands over the "TRAVEL" notice

Nan (*in a whisper*) Don't worry: I stuck a false number over the other.

She hurries out again

Bee (*looking at the phone*) Bless the woman.
Hattie I was just planning how to emigrate to Australia in the morning.
Brigadier A quite disgraceful lack of security. (*Writing*) I'll add it to the check-list for the future.
Hattie Poor Maxine. She's going to be terribly disappointed.
Brigadier We've given her the thrill of her life. Which she'll dine out on for the rest of her life.
Bee Anyway, what's a little cushioned disappointment compared (*taking up*

the travellers' cheques) to the comfort and security these will give to people who can't even afford a day trip to Margate.

Hattie Oh, yes, it's manna from heaven. I was trying to work it out in pounds, but always have difficulty with the decimal point. How much is it, Brigadier?

Brigadier (*after a moment's hesitation*) A very considerable contribution. Which can be calculated any time. Far more important to get ready for Yellow Jim.

Bee Heavens, yes! I'd forgotten all about him for the moment.

Hattie Oh, can't we have just a little sit to collect ourselves?

Brigadier No, we can't. (*Looking at his watch*) We're splendidly up to schedule, but time's as important as ammunition.

Hattie (*anxiously*) What ammunition?

Brigadier Never mind; come along, come along. Clearing Action, quickly.

They pull the sheets from the walls and start to rearrange the furniture

Hattie (*collecting the name-cards*) I'm quite sad to say goodbye to Miss Mortimer.

Bee Yes, she was very efficient.

Hattie I enjoyed her more than any of the others. I suppose because she had least to do. I think I was "behind the door" when ambition was given out. If I'd gone on the stage I'd have been perfectly happy to open doors and bring on trays.

Brigadier Then make yourself happy by opening that door for me.

Hattie opens the bedroom door

The Brigadier takes the sheets etc. into the bedroom

Bee I'm quite different. I always saw myself in a long ruby-red velvet frock smothered with diamonds at the top of a marble staircase.

The Brigadier returns

(*To the Brigadier*) How did you see yourself, suave and unattached pillar of society?

Brigadier (*huffily*) Certainly not escorting you dressed up like the dog's dinner. Come along, the sofa.

Nan comes back

Nan You're top of the pops with Maxine, Brigadier.

Brigadier Nice little woman. Did you deliver her to Mr Ashmore safely?

Nan (*nodding*) And she gave me ten pounds for your private telephone number!

Hattie Nan!

Nan (*with a chuckle*) Gave her my dentist's number. (*Serious again*) Mr Ashmore says there's little traffic, so once he's dropped her back, he wants me waiting at the front, so he can pick me up without parking. (*Starting to go*) I'd better look a bit more like I did when I worked for Jimmy boy.

Brigadier Don't be long. (*Consulting his clip-board and watch*) You should be leaving in one minute.

Act II

Nan Only two secs, then I'll go straight down. OK?
Bee Don't forget to give the warning ring when you get back.
Nan OK. Understood. Roger. Out.

She exits

Hattie Oh, dear, I wish I was like Nan. She seems to see everything so clearly. It's all behind a sort of veil to me. Especially this one.
Bee (*going to the door*) I'll make a nice, veil-lifting cup of tea.
Brigadier No, no, Beatrice: we haven't time for tea.
Bee We've time for a six-course luncheon. Tea, or Hattie and I mutiny...

She goes out

Brigadier Hurry, then. Is there something you don't completely understand, Miss Hatfield?
Hattie Shamingly, yes.
Brigadier But I briefed you all only this morning.
Hattie Yes, it's briefing that muddles me most. Couldn't you just run through it now in ordinary language?
Brigadier (*sighing deeply*) Very well. (*Consulting his notes and explaining very clearly*) Miss Parry cleaned for this Yellow Jim fellow. Clear?
Hattie Clear.
Brigadier This Yellow Jim mentioned the one thing he wanted was to meet this famous Shakespeare actor fellow. Clear?
Hattie Clear.
Brigadier Miss Parry's rung Yellow Jim to say she now works for parents of Shakespeare fellow, and that if they like this Yellow fellow, they'll arrange a meeting with their son. Clear?
Hattie A little foggy.
Brigadier So Yellow Jim (*looking at his watch*) – in two minutes fifteen seconds – will draw up in his Rolls-Royce in front of Actor's house in Kensington Church Street. Miss Parry and Mr Ashmore meet him there, say there's been a change of venue, and bring him here in the Ashmore car with some excuse about the Yellow Rolls attracting too much attention.
Hattie Before you ask: freezing fog's descended. Why didn't he come here straight away?
Brigadier (*horribly patient*) Because he mustn't have this address, or he'd be able to trace us. With Mr Ashmore bringing him to the back entrance, and Miss Parry telling him the fifth floor but pressing third floor button, and then taking him the long way round – heavens! I must put the dud bulb in the corridor. (*He hurries to the desk, takes out a bulb, and goes into the hall to the front door*)
Hattie (*following him round*) You haven't got to the part I really wanted to know about: mine.
Brigadier In a moment. It's essential it's dark in the corridor.

He collects a chair and goes out of the front door

At the same moment Bee comes in with the tea

Bee I've made it so strong we'll be able to sail through anything.

Hattie (*distraught*) I'd feel happier if I could just find out what boat I'm in.
Bee (*pouring out*) Yes, Bertie is inclined to complicate it a bit. (*Conspiratorially*) I'll explain quietly to you while he's out of the way.
Hattie Oh, I should be so grateful! Not what everyone else is doing: what I'm supposed to be doing.
Bee Very simple, dear. Pop stars, even more than most men, love flattery. To make him feel relaxed and safe, you pretend to be his greatest fan.
Hattie But I know more about—nuclear reactors than I do about pop.
Bee Doesn't matter in the slightest. You don't have to admire his work, just him.
Hattie But I do: that's easy.
Bee Then lay it on as thick as you like. Flattery never has, and never will, fail with any man of any age.
Hattie (*touching wood*) I hope this won't be the exception.

The Brigadier comes back with a bulb and the chair

Brigadier Could hardly find the front door myself.
Bee Splendid. Come and drink your tea.
Brigadier Remind me to put up the false door number at the last moment. Just in case he catches sight.

The front doorbell rings

(*Panicking*) It can't be them already!

As they all freeze in alarm the bell rings again

Bee (*in a whisper*) No, not the signal. You'd better see, Hattie.
Hattie Say it's the police!
Bee Of course it isn't the police. Go on.

Hattie hurries out

Brigadier (*alarmed*) The fastest timing from the actor's house to here on the dry-run was four minutes forty-eight seconds. We should have at least another three minutes.

Hattie comes back

Hattie It's Miss Meadows——

Blanche eases herself into the room

Blanche Sorry to pop in without warning, dears.
Bee (*firmly*) You'll kindly pop out again immediately. We're expecting a very important visitor.
Blanche I merely wondered if you had any more of those Chinese rags?
Bee No.
Blanche (*going to the clock*) Oh! But still have your little clock, I spy.
Bee The cheque bounced.
Blanche There'll be no trouble like that with me. I shall pay cash.
Bee You will not. You will please go, because we're in a hurry.
Blanche (*sitting*) I'm not in a hurry.
Brigadier Do you want me to ring the police, madam?

Blanche I thought you were expecting an important visitor——
Hattie (*desperately*) We are, I promise. He's due any moment.
Blanche (*smugly*) Then you don't want police here at the same time, do you? I'll skip as soon as you've sold me the clock. Look I have the money all ready: (*counting it out on to the table*) seventy pounds.
Hattie You agreed seventy-five before.
Blanche Oh, forgetful me! (*Putting down another note*) There, then. All right?
Bee (*after a moment's thought*) If you go immediately.
Blanche (*producing a paper*) As soon as you've signed the receipt.

Bee starts to sign

No, not Marie Antoinette, dear, that's my little joke.

Bee crosses out and signs

Sweet of you. Thanks everso. (*Putting the clock and the receipt in her grip*) If your important visitor has anything to sell remember me. Tooteloo . . .

She goes out

Brigadier Witch.
Hattie Your lovely clock, Dame Beatrice!
Bee We had to get rid of her. (*Innocently*) And — oh, forgetful me! I never mentioned I had an accident yesterday, and dropped it on the floor. Expect she's paid about right now.
Brigadier (*nervously*) Well, never mind that. She's made us all behindhand——

A sharp ring on the bell

(*Alarmed*) Not the right ring!
Hattie This time it really is the police!
Bee Rubbish.

The bell rings again

But we must answer. (*Gesturing to Hattie*) Quickly.

Hattie runs out

Brigadier If it's that damn rag and bone woman back again——

Mrs Marlborough marches in

Blanche It's me: Ada Marlborough.
Bee What on earth——
Mrs Marlborough Keep your 'air on, I won't be 'alf a mo'.
Brigadier You certainly won't. You'll kindly leave before——
Mrs Marlborough All right, General, all right: no need to fall off your 'orse. I just want to know: 'ave you got a cleaner yet?
Bee No, and we certainly don't——
Mrs Marlborough (*over-riding him*) And I certainly don't want to come. So don't get aereated. But I've just got a job (*gesturing*) with the lady upstairs——
Hattie Mrs Marlborough, please——

Mrs Marlborough (*over-ridingly*) Listen! And if you don't tell 'er — what you found out about me when I came to see you, I'll pop down and give you a blow through once a month, free!

Bee We don't want you to blow through——

Mrs Marlborough But you'll keep mum?

Bee If you'll go immediately.

Mrs Marlborough I'm gone. But remember — if you do the dirty on me — (*looking ceilingwards*) — I can make your lives 'ell with me 'oover. Tat-ta . . .

She goes out

Brigadier Quickly, quickly: they'll be here any moment.

Bee I'll get my wrap. Weren't you going to wear a dressing-gown, Bertie?

Bee exits into the bedroom

Brigadier Of course, of course! Be darkening the room, Miss Hatfield.

He hurries out

Hattie starts pulling the curtains

Bee comes back with a shawl and wearing dark glasses

Bee Wait a minute, I can't see anything!

Hattie The Brigadier said this Yellow fellow mustn't be able to recognize the room.

Bee The Brigadier isn't the one supposed to be suffering from weak eyes; I don't want a broken leg as well. (*She switches on the table lamp*) All right now.

Hattie closes the curtains

The Brigadier hurries in wearing dressing-gown, slippers and a smoking hat

Brigadier (*going to the desk*) Zero hour! Quickly! Finish the furniture while I do the number. (*He takes a false number from the desk drawer*)

As they move the furniture to new positions, he goes out to the hall and hangs the false number on the front door

Bee (*moving an armchair with Hattie*) Dear Mother! Look at the dust. But there's the button off my favourite dress! How lovely.

Brigadier Damn your buttons. Chairs.

They move other furniture

I've decided that as I'm married to you, Beatrice, I'll have to call you "dearest".

Bee Not at all, my darling.

Brigadier Now, don't go too far!

Hattie (*picking up the stole*) Can I borrow this, Dame Beatrice? (*Shaking out her hair*) I'll feel happier with a little disguise.

There's a warning ring on the front doorbell

Act II

It's them!
Brigadier (*moving about in alarm*) Now keep calm, keep calm.
Bee Well keep calm. Sit down and be reading the paper to me. (*She hands him a newspaper*)
Hattie I must be doing something! I can't be aimless.
Bee Be arranging the flowers.
Hattie They're arranged.
Bee Then disarrange them!

She and the Brigadier sit. Hattie seizes the flowers out of the vase and starts replacing them one by one

Brigadier (*with the newspaper held close to his eyes*) It says here that lice are on the increase again.
Bee How horrible.
Brigadier Evidently the little blighters can jump from head to head.
Bee A warning not to have tête-à-têtes, eh?

The door opens and Nan appears. She has a strange hair-do with a scarf low on her forehead, and more scarves around her neck and waist

Nan I've brought him, madam. The one and only Yellow Jim!

Jim comes in. He is about thirty, dressed completely in yellow, with his own style of make-up and jewellery. He is bouncily extrovert and some part of him is always moving to unheard rhythm. He speaks exuberantly

Jim Ciao, ciao, ciao, folks!
Brigadier (*involuntarily*) My God!
Bee (*covering*) Yes, isn't it a lovely surprise to see him in the flesh, dearest?
Hattie Oh, what a wonderful honour! Ciao, ciao, ciao.
Jim (*partly masking his cockney accent with bogus Italian*) Ah! You speaka Italiano?
Hattie (*faintly*) Just a word or two.
Jim (*with a wink at her*) Same 'ere, darling. But Italy's Top of Pops now so: Viva Roma, and Bury Bermondsey!
Hattie Oh, how clever, how wonderfully clever.
Nan Well, Mr Jim, I need hardly say these are the famous parents of the famous actor.
Jim Grazie, grazie, for seeing me. Not that I can see you, darlings! Can't we have a little more luce, eh?
Brigadier It's my poor wife's eyes, Mr — er. She mustn't have strong light.
Jim You don't say! But that's awful. (*Bouncing over and kneeling beside Bee, and speaking with genuine but overdone sympathy*) Ah, pauvra Mama! You got bad eyes, eh? That's bloody awful. There, there . . . (*Kissing her*) Yellow Jim'll make you better. (*Kissing her again*) There, there, pauvra Mama.
Nan If his fans could see that, madam, they'd tear you to pieces.
Bee (*struggling faintly in his embrace*) Thank you, thank you, that's enough. I mean: I really do think I can see a little more clearly.
Nan And this, Mr Jim, is their niece, Miranda.
Jim (*going to her*) Ah, Miranda! A smashing name. Miranda. (*Crooning*)

"Mi-ran-da! Her fair hair — and her — green eyes — and her — red lips — and her — all that's Mi-ran-da." (*To Hattie*) You've given me an idea, darling. If it works your name'll be on a million records by the end of the year.
Hattie Oh, what an honour! From someone so famous. Who I think is so marvellous. Who all the world——
Nan (*loudly interrupting*) Perhaps I'd better go and start cleaning the silver, madam?
Jim (*to Bee*) Can't she stay, Mama? So long since I haven't seen her.
Bee Yes, of course: the more the safer; (*correcting*) the merrier.
Jim (*going to Nan, and putting his arm round her*) All the Junkies luvva our Mabsie. Why you leave us, Mabsie?
Nan I told you, Mr Jim: my husband got jealous.
Jim A few years younger and he might've had cause. (*To the others*) Though she gave us hell. Treated us like school-kids. We had to lock the bathroom door or she'd've been in washing us. A great bullying mama she was. We loved her. (*Hugging her*) We loved our great bullying Mama Mabsie. (*He kisses her repeatedly*)
Nan (*excusingly*) It's all right, madam. He's into Universal Love.
Jim Yes, I luvva everyone. (*Singing in a long drawn-out, high-pitched tone*) "Everyone-should-luvva-everyone." (*Going to Hattie*) Isn't that right, Miranda?
Hattie Oh, yes, it is right. Very, very right.
Jim Ah, cara piccola Miranda! (*Kissing her*) I luvva her, too.
Hattie Everyone should love everyone. (*She pecks him back*)
Jim Yes, there must be love in the world. I love everyone. And you, Papa. (*Kissing the Brigadier*) Caro Papa.
Brigadier Now, just a moment, just a moment——
Bee (*quickly*) Yes, perhaps we'd better discuss what you came about.
Jim You got sense, Mama. I shouldn't even be here. My Junkies are in the studio waiting to record. We must be quick, subito!
Brigadier Well, we understand from — er——
Nan Mabs Naismith.
Brigadier —from Mrs Naismith, that you are a great admirer of our boy.
Jim (*as genuine as he can be*) Si, si, you're right. Bloody right. He's my idol, Papa. I see him as Macbeth. I see him as Hamlet. I see all his plays. What style, eh. What elegance. What personality. Bloody marvellous. Superbo!
Brigadier I have to say I find your admiration a little surprising.
Jim No, no, Papa. I dress up like this: you think I'm a fool——
Brigadier No, no.
Hattie The complete opposite.
Jim I didn't have no education, Papa, but I'm not stupido. I make a million, piu, meno, every year. But — for how much longer, eh?
Nan Now, Mr Jim, none of your gloomy act.
Jim When all the fans screamed and yelled, it was easy. Now they listen, it's a strain. At the end of a gig I feel kinda — antique.
Hattie Oh, you poor, poor boy.
Jim (*going and putting his arm round Hattie*) Si, Miranda understands. Don't you, darling? I worry about what's going to happen in the future. So what do I think Miranda, eh?

Act II 53

Hattie Everyone should love everyone. (*She pecks him*)
Jim Thanks. (*Explaining clearly*) I think: why not go straight, eh? Start in a play with a big star, so it'll be stupendo. While I'm still famous, so they think I'm stupendo. Then slowly get stupendo, and maybe play Hamlet myself one day.
Bee You'd be wonderful. It's a very clever idea, Jim. Very clever.
Hattie Yes, very clever. Though the loss to pop——
Bee (*quickly*) Will be the theatre's gain.
Jim You think so, everyone?
Bee I'm sure so.
Hattie I'm sure so, too.
Brigadier (*pointedly*) If you had our boy helping you.
Jim Ah, now you come to it, Papa! Would he, eh? That's the point. Would he?
Bee I think he could be persuaded. You see, he's in much the same situation: getting older, not so many classics he can play safely——
Brigadier That's why he's so delighted with this modern play he's found. A marvellous part for him.
Bee And there's this other marvellous part of an ex-pop star: that really could have been written for you, now we see you. Famous, good-looking——
Hattie Gentle, but a real man——
Bee Exactly.
Hattie With enormous personality and strength of character——
Bee Quite.
Hattie Magnetism flowing from every———
Bee (*hastily taking over*)—from everywhere, yes. And a lovely dying scene at the end. Would you play it for him?
Jim Would I, darling? Mio Dio! I'd pay to do it.
Brigadier There's no question of that of course. (*A little too casually*) Though—if you've money to spare—production expenses being so enormous these days—he might be glad of a little more capital.
Jim Bene, bene, Papa. As much as he wants. Our money boys can meet and fix it.

Slight pause while they wonder how to proceed

Bee The only trouble I see is: will he believe you really mean what you say?
Brigadier Of a different generation, he's a bit suspicious of pop folk. Says they'll never put their money where their mouth is.
Jim Then we show him, Papa. Simplicee. (*Pulling out his cheque book*) How much you want?
Bee I suppose a sort of little deposit might influence him.
Jim Then we will influence him, darling. How much? Three or four grand?

Bee looks puzzled

Nan Thousands, madam.
Bee Oh, well, yes, three or four (*hopefully*) or five.
Jim You're right again, Mama. Cinque. My lucky number. It'll only go to the bloody tax-man otherwise. (*Going to the table*) What name?

Brigadier The Company hasn't got a name yet. Make it out to Bearer.
Jim Bene, bene. (*Writing*) Cinque mille sterlino.
Bee The trouble is: he's so vague. He'll probably lose the cheque. (*To Brigadier*) Far better if we get the money for him, dearest. (*To Jim*) could you scribble a note to the bank authorizing payment in cash?
Jim Certo, certo, Mama. Anything to please you and him, and get me in.
Bee I think we could almost guarantee that now. We'll arrange a meeting, and let you know.
Jim Then I leave it all to you, Mama. (*Approaching Bee*) Because you're sweet and clever and kind. Like a great wise Buddah. That's it, a Buddah. (*Crooning*) "A mama who's a Buddah — a great wise and lovely Buddah — a Buddah the whole world would like to own" — (*to Bee*) I'll see you're on a million records, too, Mama. (*Kissing her*) I luvva you. I luvva you all. (*Kissing Hattie*) I luvva piccola Miranda. (*Kissing the Brigadier*) I luvva Papa. And I luvva Mama Mabsie. Come on, Mabsie: my Junkies'll go bananas if I don't get to the studio. So I'll show you how much I luvva you in the car.

He goes out crooning "A mama like a Buddah". Nan follows, with a "thumbs-up" sign

Bee (*removing her dark glasses*) I feel quite guilty. It was like taking milk from a baby.
Brigadier There's obviously plenty more milk in that particular bottle. (*Pulling the curtains*) Turned out quite a decent fellow — except for that disgusting kissing.
Hattie (*who is lying back dreamy-eyed*) I thought it was marvellous. Blissful. I haven't enjoyed myself so much since I spent all night under an oak in Richmond Park forty years ago. (*Dreamily*) And I'm not sure that was as good, because there was a heavy dew, and we both got decidedly damp. Damn Nan.
Bee Whatever for?
Hattie Think of her in the back of the car with him.
Bee Before little Miranda's imagination runs away with her altogether do you think she could make us some fresh tea?
Hattie (*hurriedly collecting the pot*) Yes, yes, of course, I'm so sorry. I don't know what came over me. Please forget about Richmond Park. It must have sounded awful. But I must tell you: nothing — happened. (*Sighing deeply*) Unfortunately.

She goes out

Brigadier (*darkly*) I think we've got to be a little careful about Miss Hatfield.
Bee (*sinking into a chair*) And me, if it comes to that. Five thousand's marvellous. But it's left me completely exhausted.
Brigadier (*sitting*) Can't say I feel quite so on form myself.

The telephone rings

Bee Oh, drat the thing. For once I agree with you, Bertie: let it ring.
Brigadier No; there may be some hang-up over Yellow Jim's return.

Act II							55

Bee You cope then; I'd be as inadequate as Hattie.
Brigadier (*going to the phone*) Wish Miss Parry was here . . .

At that moment Nan comes in

But, my God, you shouldn't be! Has something gone wrong?
Nan I left when I passed him over to Mr Ashmore. He started going too far, so I said I had a milk-pudding in the oven.
Brigadier You must follow the plans! (*Mollified*) Never mind: means you can answer that.
Bee As there's no danger just put them off.
Nan OK. (*Taking up the phone and speaking with an accent*) Instilute of Oliental Studies. Oh, so solly. Long number. (*She puts down the receiver*)
Bee (*laughingly*) Don't you ever get tired, Nan?
Nan I do, and am. But I feel it's so marvellous we can accomplish something like the annexe so late in life, that I rise above it.
Bee Yes, it's wonderfully satisfactory to prove that age isn't limiting so long as one——

The telephone rings again

Brigadier (*worried*) They're so persistent: it must be something urgent. Better answer, Miss Parry.
Bee If it's me, I'm having my toes done.
Nan (*into the phone*) Dame Beatrice's residence. (*She listens*) No, I'm sorry, Dame Beatrice has just gone out.
Bee Who is it?
Nan (*into the phone*) But I'm sure will want to know who rang? . . . Who? . . . I'm so sorry, I still haven't quite got it. Mrs Habib?
Bee (*getting up*) Mrs Habib! Heavens, I want to speak to her.
Nan Oh, what luck; she's just come back to fetch her umbrella. Hold the line.
Bee (*into the phone*) Yes, Mrs Habib, dear? . . . Oh, how exciting! . . . Splendid. Thank you so much. Goodbye. (*She puts down the phone*) My nice Lebanese lady I clean for.
Nan I thought she had a funny accent. I must try to remember it.
Brigadier (*suspiciously*) What was so exciting?
Bee Uum——

Hattie returns with the tea

Hattie Sorry to have been so long, but I was making myself mint-tea. More calming. (*She pours out*)
Brigadier (*accusingly*) You're up to something, Beatrice.
Bee (*after a moment*) In a sort of way, yes. And as it's come up now, perhaps you'd better know about it now. Will you get your tea and sit. Because I think it's going to be a bit of a shock.
Hattie Oh, Dame Beatrice, I can't stand another at the moment.
Bee It's all right, dear: a nice shock.
Brigadier (*crossly*) Then administer it without any further preamble, Beatrice.

Bee Very well. (*Urgently*) I'm so longing to get the annexe open, and our friends comfortably installed——
Nan Not more than we are, Dame Beatrice.
Brigadier Would we have risked two operations in one afternoon otherwise?
Bee Yes, yes, we do all we possibly can. But much as I hate to admit it, I think we're all getting a bit tired.
Hattie But we must go on. We must get them settled in.
Bee Which in itself will mean a great deal of work. So before that, what we need is a really good rest.
Brigadier We've got it: no other operation for eight days.
Bee I mean more than that, Bertie. So, if what I was talking to Mrs Habib about comes off—(*joyfully*)—we're all going to Monte Carlo for a long weekend.
Hattie Monte Carlo!
Nan We're what?
Brigadier You certainly need a rest when you come up with a mad idea like that, Beatrice.
Hattie Monte Carlo's miles away!
Bee But has lovely sun, balmy air, delicious food, and the mimosa will be out.
Brigadier You'd better see the doctor, Beatrice.
Bee It'll cost quite a lot, but our charing's earned us quite a lot——
Brigadier (*rising*) I think we'll conclude this meeting.
Nan (*also rising*) Yes, tomorrow we may all feel a bit different.
Hattie (*rising*) If you'd like to go to bed early, Dame Beatrice, I'll bring you some Oxo on a tray.
Bee (*firmly*) Sit down again, all of you, at once.

They sit

I knew this would be your reaction: that's why I never mentioned it before.
Hattie (*piteously*) Explain a little more clearly, Dame Beatrice.
Bee I will if you'll all stop interrupting.
Nan I swear not to say a word.
Hattie And I.
Brigadier Very well.
Bee Well, it really starts with (*pointing*) the large flat downstairs——
Brigadier Good God, we haven't even got enough for the next door one yet!
Nan (*warningly*) We promised, Brigadier.
Bee The remaining lease of that downstairs flat is for sale. The asking price is eighty-five thousand pounds. But as they've had no offers, I understand they'd be willing to accept eighty thousand pounds. Are you with me?
Brigadier With you. But what the devil——
Bee (*over-riding him*) Good. Now, I clean in the mornings for Mrs Habib, my charming and very wealthy Lebanese lady——
Nan Who just rang up?
Bee Exactly. And one day she told me she had a sister-in-law: a Mrs Ahmed, with a large family in Beirut.
Hattie Oh, dear, it's getting complicated.

Act II 57

Bee No, the names aren't important. But this Mrs Ahmed — even richer than Mrs Habib — is terrified about the situation there, and extremely anxious to get out of Beirut.
Brigadier Only a diplomat wouldn't understand that.
Bee So she begged Mrs Habib to find her a large flat in London.
Nan I begin to see light!
Brigadier More than I do.
Bee (*slowly*) I have told Mrs Habib that I know of an eminently suitable flat——
Hattie (*excitedly*) If she has eighty thousand pounds?
Bee No. If she has a hundred thousand pounds! (*Slowly*) We buy it for eighty thousand, and immediately sell it to Mrs Ahmed for a hundred thousand.
Nan Thereby making twenty thousand!!
Bee (*nodding*) Which would finish buying and furnishing the Spanager flat, and lend us anything we're short of for our holiday.
Brigadier (*bursting out*) You talk about these thousands of pounds, Beatrice——
Bee (*over-riding him again*) They're nothing to wealthy Lebanese who store away such sums, in cash, as funk money.
Hattie Funk money?
Bee Money ready to help them escape to safety in emergency.
Nan I see it all! If we could actually lay hands on this funk money——
Brigadier (*interrupting impatiently*) Yes, if, if, if. But the whole idea's absurd. Not only absurd, but also extremely dangerous.

The front doorbell rings

Bee Whether you're right, we shall now see, Bertie. Be a dear and open the door, Nan?

Nan goes and opens the door

Mrs Ahmed, who is enveloped in a black flowing robe, with gold showing everywhere, comes in

Mrs Ahmed?

Mrs Ahmed nods and smiles widely showing gold teeth

Mrs Ahmed Oui!
Bee (*speaking slowly and clearly*) You have brought the money?
Mrs Ahmed (*nodding and beaming*) Oui!
Bee One hundred thousand?
Mrs Ahmed (*nodding and beaming*) Oui! (*She produces a small suitcase, opens it, and shows it packed with British banknotes*)
Bee (*turning to Hattie*) Miss Mortimer, dear, could you ring up and book a weekend for four in Monte Carlo?
Mrs Ahmed (*with a strong accent*) I have friend. You find also like appartement for her?
Bee (*after a moment's delighted realization*) Oh, yes, I think we might manage that. (*Waving her to a seat*) I'll be with you in a moment, Mrs Ahmed.

(*Radiantly to Hattie*) Then, dear efficient Miss Mortimer, draw up a further list of friends needing accommodation, will you? (*With a glance at Mrs Ahmed*) I somehow feel we're soon going to be able to have another annexe . . .

Nan joyously bursts into "Vissi d'arte, vissi d'amore" as——

The CURTAIN *falls*

FURNITURE AND PROPERTY LIST

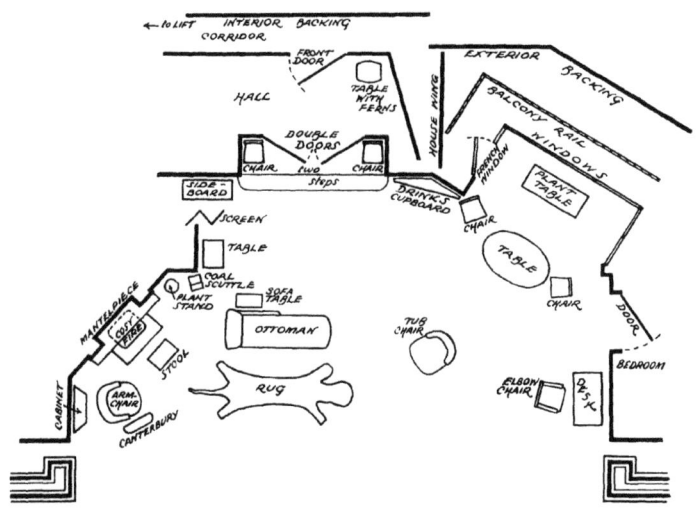

ACT I

SCENE 1

On stage: Sofa
Armchairs. *Draped over one:* shawl
Dining-table
4 chairs
Desk. *On it:* telephone, papers, letters
Desk chair
TV set
Small table. *On it:* hand-bell, lamp
Wall-shelves. *On them:* copper, brass, silver, small clock
High stool. *On it:* duster for Bee
Cleaning items—bucket, dusters, *etc.*
Window curtains (open)
Carpet

Only essential items are listed above; others may be added at the Director's discretion to emphasize the overcrowded nature of the room.

Off-stage: Chinese coat (**Hattie**)
Cheque (**Brigadier**)

Personal: **Hattie:** notepad and pen
Nan: notepad and pen
Mrs Marlborough: diamond brooch
Brigadier: letter and pen in pocket
Blanche: money pinned under clothing

Scene 2

Strike: All cleaning items

Set: Carafe of water, 4 glasses, pile of papers and files on dining-table

Off-stage: Cigarette, dusters, polish (**Bee**)
Tray with glasses of whisky (**Brigadier**)

Personal: **Brigadier:** gavel, pocket-watch; half-moon spectacles, yellow and white dusters in pocket (*for butler outfit*)
Hattie: notebook
Mrs Seymour Williams: handbag with money, envelope, address/notebook

ACT II

Strike: Carafe, tray, all glasses, files, dusters, gavel

Set: All furniture except desk, table and 3 chairs against walls
Walls hung with dust-sheets. *On sheets:* travel posters, map of world
Desk, chair LC. *On desk:* neat piles of paper, typewriter, "MISS MURIEL MORTIMER" notice, newspaper. *In drawer:* light-bulb, false number notice
Table, chair RC. *On table:* green baize, bowl of flowers, "CRUISE MANAGER" notice, clip-board, notepad, pen, hand-bell, "TRAVEL BY APPOINTMENT ONLY" notice (lying flat). *On chair:* fur stole
Chair in front of table
Button on floor

Off-stage: Potted palm (**Bee**)
Potted palm (**Brigadier**)
Notepad, pencil (**Hattie**)
Tray with cups, saucers, teapot, milk, sugar, spoons (**Bee**)
Small suitcase containing money (**Mrs Ahmed**)

Personal: **Hattie:** carpet wrapped round underneath coat; upswept glasses (*for secretary outfit*)
Brigadier: pocket-watch, tie-pin, envelope in pocket
Maxine: handbag containing rosary, travellers' cheques, pen, notepad
Blanche: bag containing money, paper
Bee: shawl, dark glasses (*for actor's mother's outfit*)
Jim: jewellery, cheque book
Mrs Ahmed: gold jewellery

LIGHTING PLOT

Practical fittings required: table lamp
Interior. The same scene throughout

ACT I, SCENE 1. Morning
To open: General interior lighting
No cues

ACT I, SCENE 2. Noon
To open: General interior lighting
No cues

ACT II. Afternoon
To open: General interior lighting

Cue 1	**Hattie** starts pulling curtains *Dim lights*	(Page 50)
Cue 2	**Bee** switches on table lamp *Snap on table lamp and covering spot*	(Page 50)
Cue 3	**Brigadier** opens curtains *Bring up general lighting to previous level*	(Page 54)

EFFECTS PLOT

ACT I

Cue 1	**Bee:** "... to buy the flat?" *Doorbell rings*	(Page 4)
Cue 2	**Bee:** "... that's all right." *Doorbell rings*	(Page 4)
Cue 3	**Brigadier:** "... proved military procedure." *Telephone rings*	(Page 9)
Cue 4	**Nan:** "... asking subversive questions." *Long doorbell ring*	(Page 11)
Cue 5	**Brigadier:** "What do I do?" *Doorbell rings*	(Page 11)
Cue 6	**Hattie:** "... is very vulnerable——" *Telephone rings*	(Page 21)
Cue 7	**Hattie:** "... flat on the floor." *Telephone rings*	(Page 27)
Cue 8	**Bee:** "I've had it since——" *Telephone rings*	(Page 28)
Cue 9	**Nan:** "... everything'd go all right——" *Doorbell rings*	(Page 28)
Cue 10	**Brigadier:** "I beg your pardon, madam?" *Doorbell rings*	(Page 28)
Cue 11	**Brigadier:** "James, I think." *Doorbell rings*	(Page 28)
Cue 12	**Mrs Seymour Williams:** "... I really must insist——" *Telephone rings*	(Page 35)
Cue 13	**Bee:** "... about the spiders. Umm ..." *Telephone rings*	(Page 35)

ACT II

Cue 14	As Curtain rises *Telephone rings*	(Page 39)
Cue 15	**Brigadier:** "... 'Operation Centre Court'." *Telephone rings*	(Page 41)
Cue 16	**Bee** (*correcting*): "Donor." *Doorbell rings*	(Page 41)

Autumn Manœuvres

Cue 17	**Brigadier:** "... he catches sight." *Doorbell rings*	(Page 48)
Cue 18	**Brigadier:** "... be them already!" *Doorbell rings*	(Page 48)
Cue 19	**Brigadier:** "... all behind-hand——" *Sharp ring on doorbell*	(Page 49)
Cue 20	**Bee:** "Rubbish." *Doorbell rings*	(Page 49)
Cue 21	**Hattie:** "... a little disguise." *Doorbell rings*	(Page 50)
Cue 22	**Brigadier:** "... so on form myself." *Telephone rings*	(Page 54)
Cue 23	**Bee:** "... so long as one——" *Telephone rings*	(Page 55)
Cue 24	**Brigadier:** "... extremely dangerous" *Doorbell rings*	(Page 57)

MUSIC USE NOTE

Licensees are solely responsible for obtaining formal written permission from copyright owners to use copyrighted music in the performance of this play and are strongly cautioned to do so. If no such permission is obtained by the licensee, then the licensee must use only original music that the licensee owns and controls. Licensees are solely responsible and liable for all music clearances and shall indemnify the copyright owners of the play(s) and their licensing agent, Samuel French, against any costs, expenses, losses and liabilities arising from the use of music by licensees. Please contact the appropriate music licensing authority in your territory for the rights to any incidental music.

IMPORTANT BILLING AND CREDIT REQUIREMENTS

If you have obtained performance rights to this title, please refer to your licensing agreement for important billing and credit requirements.

www.ingramcontent.com/pod-product-compliance
Ingram Content Group UK Ltd.
Pitfield, Milton Keynes, MK11 3LW, UK
UKHW020833050526
12271UKWH00019B/276